Living Free

NEVA COYLE

BETHANY HOUSE PUBLISHERS
Minneapolis, Minnesota 55438
A Division of Bethany Fellowship, Inc.

Copyright © 1981
Neva Coyle

Published by Bethany Fellowship, Inc.
6820 Auto Club Road, Minneapolis, Minnesota 55438

Printed in the United States of America

Library of Congress Cataloging in Publication Data

Coyle, Neva, 1943-
   Living free.

    1. Coyle, Neva, 1943-   . 2. Christian biography—United
States. 3. Depression, Mental. I. Title.
BR1725.C687A34   280'.4 [B]   81-3811
ISBN 0-87123-346-0   AACR2

Dedication

To Lee.
As we press on to the summit of our life together,
this pause to look at how much of the mountain
we've already conquered
has made me glad that we are making the climb together.

Love,
Neva

Acknowledgments

Special thanks to Joy Class for typing the original manuscript and encouraging me with suggestions and prayer, and to Nancy Shea for the cover photograph.

About the Author

Neva Coyle, founder and president of Overeaters Victorious, lives in California with her husband and three children. She was born in Redlands, California, and educated in California and Minnesota. She attended Rasmussen School of Business and Lakewood Community College.

She is the co-author of the bestseller, *Free To Be Thin*, and has also prepared a Study Guide to accompany the book.

Chapter one

Standing alone, I looked out the picture window in my living room. The quiet dark waters of the lake were still untouched by the breezes of the summer morning.

As I contemplated the day ahead of me, a familiar "heaviness" settled in upon me. Where had everything gone wrong? Why was I destined to be left out of life? It seemed to me that everyone was involved in something important—everyone except me, that is. Nothing of any consequence ever happened at our home.

Instead there was
    laundry to be done,
        dishes to be washed,
            beds to be made, and
                little noses to be wiped.

I breathed deeply; and with each breath I inhaled despair and depression, drawing them even deeper into my inner being. I had no plan or schedule for the day—or for that matter, any other day. As usual I would merely take things as they came, which included spending a good part of my day in the bathroom humoring a very upset stomach that had been with me constantly since February.

"If only things could be the way they were before . . ." I sighed in despair as I grasped for the feelings which accompany good memories.

If only I hadn't had to leave my job;
    If only I weren't pregnant;
        Everything could be all right if only. . .
        What did I do to deserve this?

"Mommy, I'm hungry."

My thoughts returned quickly to the present to face my five-year-old daughter. "Why do you always wake up so crazy early?" I snapped.

Ignoring my impatience, she climbed onto the kitchen stool as I fixed a quick breakfast of pre-sweetened cereal for her. Sheer willpower kept me from throwing up on the table. I thought I could make it into the bathroom, but just as I started toward the door my husband quietly but firmly closed it behind him. I swore under my breath. I could hear him turn on the radio, and then the electric shaver hummed out its little tune. I returned to the kitchen sink and, bending over, promptly lost everything that was willing to come up.

"You sick, Mommy?"

"What does it look like?" I muttered.

Picking up the dishrag, I washed off my face and began to lay out breakfast for my husband, Lee. I was grateful that he didn't insist on eating a big breakfast every morning. I glanced at my little daughter. I could see that I had hurt her. She didn't know what was going on.

I remembered my courtship time with Lee. How much I thought I had loved him! But, of course, then there was no way of knowing how I would be feeling nine years later.

Lee and I had spent a lot of time together by the lake in front of my parents' home. Sinking into a chair by the breakfast table, I looked back across all those times and selected one particular evening on which to focus my reflection.

Lee and I had been dating about five months, and it was a very different relationship from those I had had with other men. Lee had not once made a move to show me any physical expression of affection. I was puzzled. In the past my experience had been with fellows who were too fast, but this was my first experience with someone who was "too slow."

"I don't know," I told my mother early one evening. "If he doesn't at least attempt to hold my hand tonight, I think I'll have to drop the relationship."

"Don't be too hasty," was her advice. "He's such a nice man."

I saw in that moment the difference. I had been dating boys before. Leland was a man.

We spent a nice evening together, going out to dinner and then riding around the city to places I had never before seen. We arrived home, and as Lee walked me to the house, he caught my hand. I looked at him, but he didn't return the glance. At the door he simply took me in his arms and kissed me tenderly.

He held me for just a moment while he whispered, "I've wanted to do that for a long time, honey."

"And I've wanted you to for just as long," I said.

We said good night and he left.

My mother knew that the evening had been a good one by the look on my face as I closed the door and leaned against it weakly.

"Did he finally hold your hand?" She was teasing me.

"Um-hum," was my answer. I knew I was in love.

"Mommy, can I have some more orange juice?" I moved to the refrigerator and back, hardly even noticing where I was as my reverie continued.

Lee and I saw each other at church, where we both attended, and at least once a week outside of church after that. Those precious moments in the car before we came in were so important to me. Other fellows would have tried to make the most of it, but I never felt rushed, or pushed, or in danger of any kind of compromise in those moments with Lee. Sometimes we just talked while we sat facing each other. Other times we held hands in silence. This was different—I knew that for sure.

One of those evenings was late in the summer when the moon was full. We could hear the water lap gently on the shoreline. The silence was broken by a startling statement.

"I love you," I said.

The silence which previously had been beautiful and special became awkward and lengthy. I studied the shadow of a tree branch on the windshield of Lee's car.

After much thought, Lee answered simply, "Thank you."

I bit my lip, wishing I had never revealed my feelings. He didn't love me. Now what was I going to do? I was determined not to cry.

Our good-night kiss at the door was quick and without words. I fled into the safety of the dark house and Lee escaped into his car. I ran into my bedroom and went to the window, where I could see him drive out the driveway. He backed up and stopped. What did he do that for? I wondered. He blinked the headlights at me, and a rush of gladness and joy returned. I laughed out loud in the darkness and quickly switched the lamp on and off again in response to his signal. I easily convinced myself that Lee loved me and just didn't realize it yet, so the dating relationship continued.

Rubbing my hand wearily across my eyes, I looked around the shoreline at the opposite side of the bay. The lights in the house across the way went on.

"I wonder if they have any problems," I thought to myself as I returned to my reflections.

I had moved into an apartment with some other girls. One of my roommates was determined to make me see that a one-sided relationship meant trouble for me and dourly predicted much unhappiness ahead.

Early in the summer I began having severe headaches. I was frantically trying to make ends meet on $37.50 a week, paying $25.00 for my share of the apartment and $5.00 for my share of the groceries. I had $7.50 left for the week's bus fare, lunches, hair spray and other necessities. Many times I had to walk the four miles home from work because I didn't have the quarter it took for the fare.

Between my tight financial situation and my roommate's constant warnings about marriage to Lee, I was in a bit of emotional turmoil. I wanted to move back home to my parents' house, but they were doing some major construction, and there was just no room. Lee was more uncertain than ever about his feelings for me.

I began receiving letters from a boy I had dated in California before moving to Minnesota two years before. He asked me to reconsider a relationship with him. Now I was in a real dilemma. Lee didn't love me, he said, and the other fellow said he did. But I loved Lee and was only fond of the other fellow. Lee didn't want the added pressure of competition. My roommate nagged and harped at me constantly. The headaches became unbearable.

"Get out of my life," I finally told Lee.

"Leave me alone!" I had screamed at my roommate.

I ended up in the hospital. In the quietness of the hospital, under sedation, I tried to make some decisions about my life. I was nineteen years old. I wondered about trying to go away to college, if I could get in. My father thought it was a possibility, and we would talk about it when I got well.

"Neva, dear, here are some pretty flowers for you." The nurse brought them in and set them down on the bedside table. "Here's a card. Want me to read it?"

My heart pounded with excitement—they might be from Lee!

"No, thank you," I said. "I'll read it myself."

My thoughts were in turmoil. I was afraid to open it. What if Lee had decided to end the relationship after all? But what if the flowers were not from Lee but from my mother?

I opened the card slowly.

"I love you" was the message. It was signed, "Lee." The emotions that were so strong inside me before I read those words had now been replaced with peace.

"Over" read the little word down in the corner of the card, almost escaping my eye. "If you want to see me, please tell a nurse to call me and I'll come."

I had been without a phone, and so rang for a nurse, who made the call to Lee. When he finally came he sat on my bed and put his arms around me and I cried. He held me and then said it out loud, "I love you, Neva." We had dated a year and a half before I heard those long-awaited words.

Chapter two

In a few days I was ready to leave the hospital and I went to stay with my sister. My parents were making room for me at home, but they were not quite finished. Lee came to see me at my sister's.

"I know how I feel about you this minute," Lee said. "Do you?"

"Yes, Neva. I love you. But I can't promise how I'll feel a year from now or five years from now. If you can accept that, I want you to be my wife."

I put my arms around his neck and held him tight. After a few minutes he said, "Does that mean yes?"

"Yes," I said. "Yes!"

We were married in a private ceremony a few weeks later. I was feeling better and better, and I was sure that everything would certainly be happy-ever-after. It usually worked that way, didn't it?

I was completely convinced that my love for him was so deep and pure it would make up for anything that he lacked in feeling for me. I knew even though we came from such different family situations, it wouldn't matter because we would start our own family, cutting ourselves off completely from any background that could cause difficulty between us. I believed the old saying: "Love conquers all."

Before we were married I had worked full time in a department store selling women's clothing which I could not afford to wear. I hated it—every minute. I wanted life to be totally different once I married Lee. I wanted to give home-making a full effort. I wanted to quit my job or at least reduce my schedule to part time.

"I will be the perfect wife," I glibly reasoned. "I will putter and bake, and sew and do all the fun things housewives do." I began to cut work whenever I could until cutting back to part time was no big decision either for myself or my employer. I had those headaches again and was out sick at least two days a week.

So when I went to my employer and asked to have my schedule rearranged, he was courteous and made it very easy. The firm suggested I quit.

I put my full efforts into all the fun things housewives do (at least what I thought they did). In fact, I tried all the fun things so much that I didn't have time for the routine ones, such as making the bed, doing the dishes and the laundry. If I could fit the task into the "playing house" attitude that I had, it would get done. If not, it didn't.

I could see the disillusionment in my new husband's face almost every time he came home. I tried not to think about it. I baked and cooked and began to eat most afternoons away while I watched the soaps on TV.

Newspapers stacked in the corner of the room, shirts hung on the doorknob of the closet, the dresser top continually cluttered, socks always on the floor and under the bed. Back and forth the biting comments flew. Rarely did a day go by but that we exchanged words over small issues which carried large irritations—angry words that cut, hurt, and could never be taken back. We tried to make up with the usual words and kisses, always looking for reassurance.

"Do you love me?"

"I married you, didn't I?"

But need for reassurance deepened.

After one year in a small apartment, we bought a house in the middle of St. Paul. The upstairs of our little home had a large bedroom extending the full width of the house. We had a big dresser, a double bed, and a cedar chest, with plenty of room to walk around in besides. It was where we had our most intense moments. It was where we argued best.

"What do you mean, you don't want any children?" My attitude was as demanding as a spoiled child. "You have known since we dated how important having a child was to me. We talked about it that night in the car out by the lake. Just think about this, Mr. Coyle—no children, no marriage!" I stomped my foot and stuck out my lower lip.

Lee was quiet and serious. "I didn't say I don't want any babies. I'm saying the one I do have is quite enough."

I flew into a rage of tears and threw myself at him, pounding my fists on his chest. "How dare you! How dare you!"

Lee began to laugh. "I'm sorry, honey, but you *are* a baby—and you look so funny when you throw a tantrum!" I became exhausted, and my outburst turned to sobs. I got into bed and cried myself to sleep, keeping out of my husband's reach as much as possible.

I didn't let Lee know it at the time, but the message I got was clear. I needed to grow up, and knowing that it was the truth made it even harder to accept. I began by sheer willpower to have more of an adult attitude toward our marriage and my life.

I started looking for ways in which I could prove to Lee that I wasn't such a baby. I started to keep my house better and to cook nicer meals. I tried to be more organized in every area of my life. I began to think of ways to expose Lee to children. I wanted him to have a good feeling about kids. I had my sister's children over often for overnight stays and afternoon visits. I started to sew for them and do other things that would prove to Lee that I could in fact be a good mother. One day I saw a commercial on television asking for volunteers for foster parents. Aha! I thought, this is just what the doctor ordered. Now to approach Lee about it. I checked into the program by calling our welfare department. I found out that they paid all of the baby's expenses. I took all my data in hand and faced him.

"Honey," I said, "I've been thinking that since I'm not working and I have all this time on my hands, there should be some way to put it to good use."

"Yeah?" he said.

"I saw a commercial about a pressing need for foster parents. I was wondering how you would feel about temporarily taking care of a new baby waiting for adoption?"

"I haven't thought about it," he replied.

"I know, that's why I am talking to you about it now. Think about it for a while and we'll talk about it again, okay?"

"Okay," he agreed.

I decided to wait about three days and then ask him again.

"Honey?"

"Hmm?" from behind his newspaper.

"Have you been thinking about a foster baby?"

"Um-hmm. A little."

"Well, what do you think?"

"I think that we could look into it if you want to," he said.

"I really do, Lee. I know it would be good for us, or at least for me," I added quickly.

I made the necessary phone calls and an appointment was made for me to attend a group meeting the next week along with other prospective foster parents. The whole program was explained, and Lee and I filled out the necessary forms and consented to an inspection of our house by the fire marshall. We met with a lady called "the homefinder." She was pleasant and encouraging, expressing gratitude for our willingness to participate in the foster parents plan. In a few weeks we received a call to place a baby in our home. I was delighted. I quickly checked over the upstairs room I had prepared as a nursery. In it I had placed a small crib rescued from a closet at church. I had scrubbed it and fitted it with sheets made from some old ones I had gotten from my mother. Besides this, I had been given a bassinette that I kept in an out-of-the-way corner downstairs in the dining room.

That afternoon the baby was brought to our home. She was a little sweetheart about four days old. She slept all night the first night, and I was impressed with what a good "mother" I was going to be. None of my sister's babies had slept all night at that age. Later I found out that she was an "exceptionally good" baby (as if there is some moral quality to an infant's not being a bother!) We had her two months, and even though Lee took quite an objective attitude about the experience, we were saddened when she was placed with an adoptive family.

I called Lee at work.

"They're taking the baby today," I quavered.

"You knew it had to come sooner or later." Lee was so exasperatingly reasonable. I knew he was right.

"It is harder for me than I thought it would be," I told him.

"Well, they'll bring another one soon, won't they?"

"I hope so," I said.

After the baby left I went up to the little bedroom nursery and sat on the floor by the crib and cried.

"Maybe I shouldn't do this again," I thought. I hadn't realized it would be so hard to let the baby go.

I cleaned the room and washed the sheets, diapers, and clothes left behind. I felt strange and alone in the house. I didn't know such a little baby could be so much company.

A week later "the homefinder" called.

"Are you ready for another baby?" she asked.

"We surely are!"

"Can you be prepared by this afternoon?"

"I surely can!" I was elated.

I called Lee and told him that we would be getting another baby that day. I was surprised to hear him say, "I'm glad. I kind of miss that little extra person in the house. Call me when they bring it, okay?"

"It's another girl," I told him later on the phone. "She is not as pretty as the first one, but she is just a few days old and not very filled out yet."

She wasn't as pretty indeed—neither was she as "good." She did not sleep all night as the first baby did. She fussed. She seemed unhappy no matter what was done for or with her.

"I'm glad this is not a permanent arrangement," Lee said more than once.

"Me too," I admitted just as often.

I had to learn that a mother of a fussy baby sleeps when the baby sleeps and is up when the baby is up. I was glad when she was adopted.

There were three other babies in all. With each one Lee became more and more attached to them. The last one, a boy, stayed only a week.

"We finally get a boy and then they take him away so soon!" Was this the same man who had indicated that he didn't want any children?

He was almost afraid of the first baby, tolerant of the second, but genuinely interested in the rest of them. He would come home and head for the bassinette the first thing. He even learned to hold them.

"Is it time for us to have one of our own?" I asked cautiously one day.

"I think it is," he replied just as cautiously.

Once we had finally come to some understanding about a baby, we became truly excited about it. We had been on opposite ends of a wide spectrum and had slowly come together.

Then after having finally arrived at this momentous decision, nothing happened! So, after a while we began to consider adoption. During the time we had taken in foster babies, we had discovered we could love babies that were not biologically our own.

I was so excited when Lee said it was all right to call the adoption agency and at least begin the inquiry. We had no idea how to begin, so placing a phone call seemed like the most logical step to take.

"Children's Home Society. Good morning!" The voice of the lady on the other end of the line was cheerful and professional.

"Oh, good morning. My husband and I have been talking about adopting a baby and, well, we don't know how to begin."

"Well, you have done the right thing. I will just take your name and address. We'll send you some forms to fill out and you may return them to us."

"Okay," I said, and gave her the information.

"When we receive these forms back, we will set up an appointment for you to attend a group meeting along with other prospective parents. There you can ask all your questions and someone will be able to help you."

That was easy enough.

We quickly completed all the forms and attended the group meeting. We couldn't think of any questions to ask but took home many more forms to fill out. We went to the doctor for complete physical exams. We filled out the financial statement. We answered all the questions as best we could, and then sent them back and waited for the agency to call and set up our first appointment with a caseworker.

"Good morning, Mr. Coyle, Mrs. Coyle. I'm Lynn Hadley. I'll be handling your case." We felt instantly at ease with our young caseworker. She gave us a brief background of how adoptions were handled and asked if we had any questions.

"How long will it be before we can have our baby?" I asked.

She laughed with understanding, and assured us that it would be no longer than necessary.

During the four visits that followed, we answered questions like: Why did you get married? What first attracted you to each other? What do you love about Lee? about Neva? Do you attend the same church? Will the religion of the children be a problem to you? What do you think of discipline in the home? How do you expect to handle the child's questions about adoption? What do you think you will be like as a mother? as a father?

I looked at some of life's questions realistically for the first time, and it didn't look so bad. In fact, I looked forward to each succeeding session with our caseworker.

The questions asked during the homestudy were just what I needed for the time being to help me get my head on straight. For the first time, Lee and I examined our relationship. We looked at what we had built in the three years we had been married, how we each felt about discipline in the home, how we felt about each other and why. It was a beautiful interlude spent learning to know and appreciate each other for the first time since we had met in 1960.

In December of 1965 our daughter arrived, just two weeks after completing the four-month homestudy. Our marriage relationship was in good shape. The homestudy, under the careful hand of a competent social worker, had had a positive effect on both of us.

"Mrs. Coyle?"

"Yes."

"This is Miss Hadley."

"Oh, Miss Hadley." I was always glad to hear her voice, but something today made her sound different.

"We have a nice baby girl for you and your husband to look at."

"Really? But it's only been two weeks since we completed our homestudy. You told us it would take between two and four months."

"Is it too soon? Are you unprepared?" she asked.

"Oh, no," I said. "It's just such a surprise. A nice surprise! Oh, Miss Hadley, I think I might cry!"

"That's all right, Mrs. Coyle. I understand. You wouldn't be the first one that ever did, either. You and your husband come to the agency on Thursday at 10:00 and look at the baby. If you don't like her, or for any reason feel hesitant, it is okay. It's in no way going to hurt your chances for adoption. We'll just look for another baby. Bring some clothes with you just in case you do like her, though."

"I'm sure we'll just love her, Miss Hadley," I said.

Thursday. It was only Tuesday! We had to wait two days before we could even see her. We knew the policy of the agency was to look at the baby one day, spend about an hour or two with her, and then go home and think about it, and return the next day to get her. What a long week was ahead of us!

Chapter three

"Miss Hadley? This is Neva Coyle. I'm sorry to bother you again." I lied. I didn't care if I was bothering her again. "Have you seen the baby yourself?"

"Yes, Mrs. Coyle, I have. She's really quite a beautiful child." I didn't expect her to say otherwise.

"Well, what I was wondering was, well, we're considering the name 'Rhonda.' Do you think that would fit her?"

"Yes, Mrs. Coyle, I think that would be a perfect name for her. Anything else I can help you with?"

"No, that's all for now. See you tomorrow." TOMORROW! Not too much longer to wait. We were going to see our baby. Tomorrow!

When Lee got home we went shopping at a very exclusive children's shop to find just the right dress (pink, of course) for her to wear, plus a new blanket, white with pink appliqued animals, a lacy soft pink sweater, and little white shoes and socks with ruffles around the tiny ankles. In a flurry of excitement we took our purchases home and ceremoniously removed all the tags and packed our new little daughter's diaper bag.

We didn't talk about anything in particular; however, even the most mundane conversation that sleepless night was very special. We were going to be a family. I hadn't become the perfect housewife, but I was determined to be a perfect mother.

The next day we thought of little projects to keep us busy until time to go and visit our little one.

I manicured my nails,
      shampooed my hair,
            pressed my clothes
                  unpacked and repacked the baby's things.
Finally we got into the car and made the unbearably
long three-mile trip to the adoption agency offices. The pre-
liminary interview with the agency's director seemed an
eternity.

"Please, may I just see the baby now?" I was careful not
to say "my baby."

"Yes, Mrs. Coyle, now we'll go see her."

We walked down the hall, into a room, and over to the
crib where she was waiting. A feeling of panic gripped me,
but I managed to suppress it. "She's just a baby after all," I
tried to remind myself.

"Hi, little baby," I whispered. With one sudden motion,
she kicked her legs and stretched her arms, smiled and
cooed at us.

"Lee, look at her! She's perfect!" Suddenly my eyes
filled with tears. As I reached for her I stifled a deep sob—
her soft skin against my cheek, her weight in my arms, the
warmth of her against my breast.

"Hello, Rhonda Joy," I said. She was a delight!

At last I felt all my dreams were coming true.

Weren't they?

For a while all was well. We had our own home, which I
loved very much, and I was content with my family and
surroundings. My parents who had lost their home in a fire
about a year before were building another one in the sub-
urbs on a lovely lake where they had once lived. They were
in the finishing stages of this home when change first
threatened my life-style. Instead of finishing the house, my
parents suddenly decided to sell it and move to California
where we had lived when I was a child. I had one sister living in California already. Now another married sister and
her husband decided to move out there also. I had two
brothers, one in the military and the other still living at

home with my parents. So within a very short time my whole family had left; and I, having grown up in a large family accustomed to twenty-five or thirty people for holiday get-togethers, was left with just my husband's family.

His family was not close at all, so it really meant just Lee and my mother-in-law. I felt the impact of my family's move as if it were a death of someone very close to me.

My mother and my sister's family left first, and Dad stayed to sell the house and to take care of any unfinished business.

"Say, Pal," Lee approached me carefully. "I've been thinking." (I hated it when he called me "Pal.")

I wondered what could be coming, what could possibly happen now right in the middle of my family's move to California. Maybe he wanted to move there, too.

"What's on your mind?" I asked, giving him my attention.

"You know your folks' place is going to be worth a lot more than they're asking once it's finished." He paused to see how I was reacting so far. "It's really an opportunity for someone."

"So?" I asked.

"Honey, what do you say we buy their house?"

"Lee, how could you think such a thing?"

"Why not?" he wondered.

"Isn't it enough that I'm losing a family I am very close to?" I had never left them emotionally and didn't know how I was going to get along without them. "Not only will I be losing my mother, but I will also be living in her house. Lee, that will be a constant reminder of her. I can't do it."

He was silent, but I knew by the look on his face that nothing I said was going to change the fact that we were about to purchase my parents' house. Lee had made up his mind.

When Dad left, he drove out in his car, and I tearfully packed my mother's possessions. After crating the rest of her furniture for shipping, we signed the papers to buy the house. Next we signed the papers to sell my beloved house, packed our belongings, and moved into a yet-unfinished house I was determined to hate.

Lee was working a usual eight-hour day at first; then the overtime started. I felt so alone, except for the baby, who was starting to crawl, and the part-time carpenter who came some evenings.

I began to mourn. . .

I began to cry all the time. . .

I convinced myself that I had been handed a rotten deal.

The grieving over separation from my family had turned into self-pity. I started thinking of going to work—anything to get out of this house for a while. I reasoned that if I could earn extra money to buy some nice things for myself, maybe I could ease the pain a little.

Having been raised by Christian parents and attending church most of my life as normal routine, I had been taught a verse from the Bible that said, "For God so loved the world, that he gave his only begotten son, that whosoever believeth in him should not perish, but have everlasting life" (John 3:16, KJV). I knew that "the world" meant me, too, and also that He was promising to me everlasting life if I only would believe Him. Also I knew the promise in Revelation 3:20, "Behold, I stand at the door and knock: if any man hear my voice, and open the door, I will come in to him, and sup with him, and he with me" (KJV). I knew that I had made the conscious decision to open the door of my heart and had asked Jesus to come in and live in my heart. And true to His word, He did. I had been aware of His presence from that day on. Whenever I did anything wrong, I knew that I was not pleasing Him; and whenever I made an effort to get closer to Him, I could sense His approval as well.

Lee and I had met in church and continued to be steady attenders and faithful workers. But I had not once let Jesus soothe my pain or encourage me in any way. I liked my suffering.

I took a job three days a week cashiering in a grocery store.

I left my baby with a friend from my church who was content to stay at home and keep house and take care of her four boys. Rhonda had her middle name and she was delighted to have a baby girl around the house to play with and care for.

I enjoyed the freedom my new job gave me
from facing housework . . .
from staining woodwork . . .
from washing diapers . . .
sweeping up sawdust.

I was entering a new era in my life. I was discontented with everything and everybody. My house wasn't finished. My husband wasn't sociable enough for me. My church wasn't friendly. God seemed silent. The only thing I liked was my job, because I could stand there and chat with the ladies in my line about
nothing,
everything,
anything—
all of it unreal.

I could escape and be anything I wanted to be and it was never real. I pretended life was important and it wasn't. Only parts, at best, were of value to me. The rest of it, being constantly compared with what I thought it should be, was nothing.

All the while the discontentment was growing. I was aware of it. I began to make up excuses for it.

My furniture was not good enough.
My house was still not done.
My clothes were not nice enough.
My church was having problems.
I wanted another baby.

I did not stop to realize that discontentment is a problem in itself, coming from an incomplete relationship with Jesus Christ. I was looking to *things* for contentment. I had placed the responsibility for my happiness on things and people, forgetting that no one else can be responsible for my happiness. I looked for happiness but overlooked joy. Instead of seeking the joy which comes from within, I continued to expect happiness from external sources. I had received Jesus into my life long ago, but I was not looking to Him.

Looking back on that time, I realize now that it was like having a faucet inside the house but still running to the outside well for water, complaining all the while about the inconvenience. The absence of thankfulness in my life opened me up to discontentment. Looking to external sources caused me to think that if my furniture were only better, if my house were only done, if I could only wear nicer clothes, if my church could only solve its problems, and perhaps if we even had another baby, then I would be happy and content.

In desperation I applied for another baby; surely this second child added to the first would satisfy my needs and I would be content to stay home. But this time we were in for a long wait.

My sister and her family moved back to St. Paul and stayed with us for a few weeks. Unfortunately, this arrangement did nothing to satisfy my desire for contentment. I'm sure it didn't do much for hers either. They moved out in about three weeks.

My oldest sister and her family moved back also, into a house right down the street from me. She was having serious marital problems—problems which weighed heavily upon me, too, since I was responsible for the care of her children. It was easy for me to take on her problems, because once again I could substitute her problems for mine and ignore my feeling of uselessness. She got a job working where I did; but it wasn't so much fun for me anymore, because she knew the real me and I couldn't be as phony there anymore. My pretend time was over. I quit my job.

Chapter four

In January of 1968 I miscarried; I had not even been aware that I was pregnant. After an eleven-month delay, our adoption was complete, and we were expecting our new adopted baby any day. Nevertheless, there was a tragic sadness connected with that loss, for I think any woman who desires children would like to be pregnant with the life placed in her body by her husband, and I was no different. The doctor gave me very little encouragement of ever getting pregnant again.

A month later our Sandra came to us. She was only three weeks old but already beautiful. Surely I will be content now, I thought. But Sandra was so different from Rhonda.

She cried more,

She threw up more.

She demanded much more of my attention.

"Enough of this," I decided. "I'm going back to work."

My parents moved back to St. Paul soon after this, and I thought that having them back again would once more bring the contentment and security I had somehow lost. But it didn't. As a result I was determined to go back to work full time at the first possible opportunity.

I was also dissatisfied with my church life. I did a lot of work there, and was very active on committees, boards, and councils of every sort, each time thinking that if I accepted a new position or responsibility, I would certainly find the contentment and security for which I longed. I was sadly disappointed every time, though. Instead I grew more restless with every job I had, and began to look for ways to back out. I used the excuse that I was a born beginner, an "enthusiaser." I could initiate programs and then get others to take them over. I was proud of my ability to think up ideas, organize committees, and manipulate people. I thought it might even be my calling. I struggled for recognition, for in recognition I found some measure of

satisfaction,
contentment,
security,
acceptance,
worth—
but all temporary.

When recognition-time was over, there was a tremendous letdown:

discontentment,
disappointment,
discouragement,
depression,
despair.

And then I would start looking for another project with which to build myself up again. It was this process that led me to holding—all at one time—several jobs at church: Assistant Sunday School Superintendent, Missionary President, Church Board member, Young Adult Sponsor in the Youth Department, Choir member, Pulpit Committee, Church Librarian, Vacation Bible School Teacher, and Christmas Program Director. I made posters, decorated for the banquets, sang for the services, and almost convinced myself that I could do anything and everything better than anyone else. I was busy doing the "Lord's work," but underneath it all was a nagging dissatisfaction. I still hadn't learned that there is a subtle difference between dedication and commitment. I had given the Lord my life, I thought, but I had not given Him myself.

Something has to change, I decided.

I called the pastor.

"Pastor? This is Neva. Could I see you? It's very important. Could you come over? Tonight? Good. 7:30? Okay, that will give me time to put the kids to bed. See you then." It was a very short phone conversation. I was hoping that Pastor would not try to talk me out of the decisions I had made.

"Come in, Pastor. Lee is out for a while and it will give me a chance to talk privately. I *need* to talk to you.

"You see, Pastor," I began to select my words very carefully, "I have been feeling very discontented lately. I feel as if the whole world is having a good time and doing constructive things. I am doing nothing. Oh, I know I do quite a bit at church, but I need more. I need to do something outside, out there," I gestured toward a hypothetical horizon. "I have decided to go to work. I start next Monday looking for just the right job." I tried to reassure him with more words, "I know that God will tell me when I have found the one He has for me in His will."

Pastor didn't try to stop the stream of words, but just sat there listening as I went on, "I'll have to give up some of my responsibilities at church. You understand, don't you, Pastor? I'll have a job and my family, and you know how that is. Why, your own wife works part time, and I know you understand exactly what I'm facing."

Pastor's brow was now furrowed, and a thoughtful expression possessed his face. I rushed on before he could speak, "Before you object, please let me tell you that it also has occurred to me that I haven't many non-Christian friends, and you always are telling us to bring our unsaved friends to church. Pastor, how can I do that if I'm never out there where I can make any non-Christian friends? Think of it as sort of a missionary effort, only right here in my own city!" I hadn't thought of that before I said it, and I was impressed. Pastor wasn't.

"Have you made up your mind?" he asked.

"Yes, Pastor, I have."

"And Leland agrees?" He was too serious for me to be comfortable anymore, and I wanted him to leave.

"Oh, yes," I lied. Leland agreed only after I had twisted his arm some.

"How many responsibilities do you need to be relieved of?"

"All of them, Pastor. You understand, I don't know how demanding my new job will be, and I'll need my mind free to give it my all." I was over-enthusiastic in my efforts to convince him.

"I see." He was thoughtful and quiet as he rose to leave. "I hope you are doing the right thing, Neva."

"I am, Pastor. I'm sure of it."

Chapter five

And so it was that I quit all my jobs at church and went looking for a full-time job. In my positions at church, the recognition was short-lived and the requirements placed upon my talents and abilities were greater than the rewards and recognition I craved and received. When I get a job, I had thought, I can buy myself nice things. I can surround myself with luxuries—nice things that will tell people that I am important. I set out to secure for myself status symbols through the acquisition of material things. That would be my recognition. I would surround myself with constant reminders of my worth, of my accomplishments.

The job I got, based upon some previous experience, was clerking in a new arts and crafts shop just opening in a brand-new prestigious shopping mall close to my home. And did I have plans for that job! In just a few weeks, I had the responsibilities of the entire crafts department and did all the ordering. A few weeks later, our store severed relations with our supplier, and I was then the buyer, buying from all over the country. I took business trips to see the trade shows in hobbies and crafts. Wow! Was I thrilled!

Six months later I was offered the managership and a nice raise in salary; I was positive my dreams had all come true. I convinced myself that I had

recognition,

position,

money,

prestige

and power.

Someone else was taking care of my children, doing all the ho-hum dirty work, and I played with them in the evenings after a dinner of convenience foods purchased on my way home from work.

The store was open seventy-five hours a week. I had to be within reach all the hours I wasn't actually working. It was such an important feeling to leave a number where I could be reached whenever we went out. I really got a charge when I would receive a phone call in the middle of a party or meeting. Everyone present would be reminded, not so subtly, that

I was a MANAGER.

I was SOMEBODY.

I had ARRIVED!

Hadn't I?

Since with the manager's position came more money, the first thing to come after the increase in salary was a snappy car. The yellow convertible with white leather interior and chrome everywhere picking up my reflection reminded me again and again that I was the young woman in the yellow convertible. Feel good? You bet it did! Content? Completely! Well, most of the time. Except on my day off—or when one of the children was sick and I had to stay home. There were times late at night when I couldn't sleep. Occasionally when I would try to pray or read the Bible I felt uneasy, so I quit trying to pray or read my Bible.

After my car payment and the money I had to give Lee to set aside for my insurance and tithe, I had plenty of money left to spend as I wanted.

And I spent,

and spent,

and spent some more.

I bought anything I needed or ever would need, and all I wanted, and then spent some more. Then I opened charge accounts. I charged anything I wanted. Sometimes I charged things I didn't even want. I loved to pull out that charge card.

One day my paycheck didn't cover the payments on my charge accounts. I was briefly shaken and temporarily aware of my problems.

"Leland," I said on the next pay day, "I've decided to pay my own tithe. You always put in an offering at church for the two of us, and since I don't do any work there anymore, it makes me feel as if I don't give anything at all. So from now on I want to put in my own tithe."

"Oh, I just thought that it would make it easier for taxes if it was all put together," he said.

"I'll worry about keeping track of my own contributions so it won't be a problem."

And so the decision was made. I would pay my own tithe. And I did—to the department stores that had become my temple, to buy the *things* that had become my god.

When I should have realized that the monthly payments were only a percentage of what I owed, I was able to ignore the balance figure on the monthly statements and, in my mind, I only owed that payment. One month when I had been too busy at work to buy too many things and the statement still came with a really high payment due (because of my balance plus whatever part of the previous month's payment I hadn't made), I felt anger at the department stores for not giving me a break in the payment column.

It was necessary for me to leave work earlier those days; I had to get home before Lee did for fear he would pick up one of the statements at the mailbox. He didn't even know I had charge accounts. I knew he would be furious if he found out. He was so cautious and sensible about money, and he would never understand about my needing things. I knew he didn't like it when I occasionally worked evenings. My lunches with salesmen brought quiet opposition. He didn't understand about my business trips. The charge accounts would not go over well and I knew it.

The old discontented feelings came flooding back when I realized that I had gotten in over my head. This time there was also the nagging fear that Lee might find out. With every purchase, I vowed it would be my last until everything was brought up to date and paid in full. I felt like an alcoholic.

Would God help me? Probably not. I thought He was angry with me for my irresponsibility; and because I had not paid my tithe, I was afraid to pray. Sometimes I wondered if He felt anything at all toward me. So, again, here I was:

discontent,
alone,
and this time
scared.

"Why do I spend like this?" I wondered.

Months passed with this turmoil churning inside me. I was able to cut down on my personal spending by transferring my compulsion to the shop. I went on extravagant buying trips and bought everything I wanted and liked for the shop inventory. My employer was patient and reasonable in his request for an explanation. He again went through the procedure by which we determined how much I should spend on new inventory. I pretended that I was understanding it for the first time.

I knew that he would never understand the high it gave me to approach a supplier, especially in a distant city, and to buy as if I were backed up by Fort Knox. I felt important, secure, powerful. I was *somebody* for a while.

Then in the winter of 1971, I caught the flu like everyone else—except, not like everyone else. I did not get well in 24 hours, or 48 hours, or 5 days.

By the time I went to the doctor, I was a physical, mental, and emotional wreck. I knew that I couldn't afford to take any more time off from work. I needed to pay my charge account payments.

The doctor's diagnosis was more like a judge's verdict with a mandatory sentence:

I was pregnant—
I was destroyed!

Chapter six

I left the doctor's office, although I don't remember it. I couldn't believe what was happening to me, if it were indeed happening. I heard myself saying over and over again, "No, no!"

Driving down Maryland Avenue and north on the freeway, I fought back tears, determined not to cry.

"What will Lee say?" I wondered.

I approached my exit and made the turn. "I won't tell him," I said aloud.

"That's stupid," I thought, "he will have to know eventually. I might as well get it over with."

I did not return to work that afternoon. I went home to be alone. I wished God would speak to me and tell me what to do. But I did not ask Him. I did not pray. I did not consider talking to Him first. I just wished He would somehow talk to me.

I came home and the silence of the house was eerie to me. I turned on the television set and escaped into the world of soap-opera fantasies.

I finally managed to fix dinner and when I was setting the table, Lee came home with the girls. I settled them in front of the TV and turned on *Sesame Street*.

I went into the kitchen where Lee was going over the day's mail.

"I went to the doctor today," I said.

Lee looked at me. "That's good. You look awful."

"Thanks a lot." I was in no mood for either teasing or criticism.

"Well?" Lee was looking at me a little closer than usual.

"Well, what?"

"What did he say about you? Are you working too hard?"

"No," I said.

"Well, what is wrong?"

"Nothing is wrong. I'm pregnant."

"You're what?" His expression told me he thought I was joking and that he hoped I was.

"You heard me." My reply was without emotion. I was numb. Lee was shocked.

We faced a time of great adjustment. I knew that it would be out of the question for me to continue working full time with a small baby and two other children as well. I was afraid that the secrets I had been keeping from Lee about my charge accounts would have to come out if I lost my job right away. I pretended that I wanted to work as long as possible simply because I loved my job so much.

I was constantly nauseous. I lived in fear, and I was depressed most of the time.

The doctor gave me some pills to control the nausea, with this observation, "Most of this nausea could have an emotional base, Neva."

"Psychosomatic?" I was defensive. "Nonsense."

"Is anything bothering you?"

"Not anything I can't handle," I assured him.

"Well, whatever it is, if you ever want to talk to me about it, I'm available," he offered.

"There's nothing, really." I turned my back on help.

I wanted desperately to tell someone how I had messed up my life, but I was afraid that the doctor would inform me that I needed to tell Lee; and I knew *that* without being told. I couldn't face it, however. Not yet. I would try to straighten it out myself first. I set my jaw in determination—I would handle my own affairs. A little martyrdom came into my attitude and it gave me a slight boost. But before long it, too, had turned into bitterness. I was trying to straighten out a mess that no one else knew existed. Those close to me knew in a general sense that I had some problems; but since I would not share them with anyone, they were unable to help.

I was alone,

and it was my own doing.

The baby was due in September. That meant I had six months left to work. Six months to pay off just over a thousand dollars' worth of charge accounts at four stores.

I couldn't afford one day without pay if I were to pay all my charge accounts by the end of August.

I was supposed to be at work at nine o'clock each morning, but it was more like ten or ten-thirty most mornings during my pregnancy. I was sick both in the early morning and the late evening, and by 3:30 in the afternoon I could hardly stay awake. Although I was supposed to stay at work until 5:30, I started going home before 4:00 p.m.

The buzzer on my office phone startled me one afternoon when I had my head down on my desk.

"Hello, Mrs. Coyle here, may I help you?" I managed.

"Hello, Neva." I recognized the voice of my employer.

"Hello, Mr. Krantz," I said.

"I tried to call you this morning when I got into the office. There was no answer."

"I'm sorry. I was a little late today. Anything I can do for you now?"

We went on into a business conversation. I answered the questions he asked and he seemed satisfied with the information I gave him.

"I'm going to have to tell him," I told Lee later that night.

"Have you decided when?"

"No. I want to put it off as long as possible."

I got another call later in the week from Mr. Krantz again. "I called you yesterday afternoon, Neva. Whoever answered the phone said you had gone home early."

"Yes, I had a personal matter to attend to."

"Everything's all right, I hope," he said.

"Oh, yes. Everything is all right," I lied.

"I'll be over to see you sometime this week. I'll be leaving town and want to check with you before I go."

"Do you know when?" I asked.

"No, I don't," he said. "Is it important? Do you plan to be gone?"

"Oh, no. It's just that we like to have everything looking nice when you come. Also, our classes are in session now and it gets pretty hectic around here some days." I tried to discourage him.

"Well, my schedule is pretty indefinite, usually, but I'll be there sometime this week."

"Okay," I said. "We'll see you when you get here, then."

I gave the order to clean up the store, the office, and the classroom storeroom and went home. I knew that I would have to be there when he came and that meant any hour of the day, any day. I needed some sleep.

I managed to work all the hours I was supposed to for the next three days. Mr. Krantz came on the third afternoon.

"Everything looks real good," he told me after sort of making an inspection tour of the whole store. "I'm going to Mexico on a vacation and then to Arizona for some business. If you need anything just leave a message with my secretary. I'll be calling her every day. Otherwise, I'll see you when I get back."

"When are you leaving?" I asked.

"About six this evening," he said.

I could relax after six, I thought. I'll take tomorrow off.

I ran the store by phone for a few days after that and got some rest. I began to feel a little better. In a couple of weeks everything was going relatively smooth, even though I still felt pretty rough some of the time.

Mr. Krantz came back into town and I decided to tell him I was pregnant.

"Does this mean you'll be leaving us?" he said when I told him.

"I'm afraid so," I said. "I managed okay with two children; but working with three, and one of them just a baby—well, I don't know if I could handle that or not. The baby-sitting fee would be out of sight."

"When will you have to quit?"

I was relieved to think I could pick my own date to leave.

"The baby's due the end of September," I said. "I'd like to work until the end of August."

"I think you had better begin now to find a replacement. Do you know of anyone who would be good in your job? If we could hire someone by the first of June, you would have three months in which to teach them about the field and train them in your position."

I was very depressed at the thought of someone taking over my precious job, but I agreed that I would start looking soon.

I knew of a woman in the shopping center who had expressed some disenchantment with the company that employed her. I thought she might be right for the job. My employer felt the same way and hired her to start, much to my surprise, immediately. I deluded myself to think that I could breathe a sigh of relief. It would be easy for me now.

We worked together for five days, and Elizabeth had her signature filed at the bank with mine. I began to relax. I went to the doctor for my regular check-up one afternoon, and when I returned I was met on the sales floor with a message.

"Mr. Krantz called while you were out, Mrs. Coyle."

"What did he want?" I met the gaze of one of the sales people.

"I don't know. He talked to Elizabeth."

"How long ago did he call?" I was hoping he wouldn't be too angry with the two hours it takes for a doctor's appointment.

"Oh, I didn't mean on the phone, Mrs. Coyle. He made a personal call. He was here. He left about twenty minutes ago."

"When did he arrive?" I wanted to know.

"Right after you left," she said.

That meant he was in the store for about two hours waiting for me.

"He wants you to call him, Mrs. Coyle."

"All right, I'll do it now," I said.

I walked slowly toward my office and opened the door. I was met with cardboard boxes containing my personal things and all my furniture rearranged, all my desk drawers open, and the new manager-to-be settling in. The phone call to my employer confirmed my worst fears.

"Neva," he began, "I'm concerned about how things are going there."

"Yes, sir."

"Sales are down, your inventory is too high, and you've been missing quite a bit of work. You were at the doctor?"

"Yes, but I'm fine. It was just a routine visit."

"I see." He was looking for just the right words. "Well, good. I'm glad you are all right."

"Thank you, Mr. Krantz."

"Neva, since business has been slow, the payroll has to be cut down even more than you cut last week."

We had adjusted payroll by reducing sales-help hours, but I knew we were as low as we could go. I looked around at my office and all my personal belongings not-so-tactfully out in the open for all to see.

"Neva?"

"Yes," I said.

"I have to cut starting from the top. You understand."

"Yes, sir," I said, but I didn't.

"I can't afford both Elizabeth and you, too. And as long as you are leaving in a few weeks anyway. . . well, we'll have to make it sooner."

"When? May I finish out the week, Mr. Krantz?"

"We just can't afford it, Neva. You can leave now."

I was fired.

I was sick.

I was angry.

I was scared.

I walked into a quiet house and sat in the stillness. I was determined not to cry. After a while I turned on the television and escaped into the safety of made-up problems. I laid on the couch and went to sleep with the make-believe world of the soap-operas still on the screen.

Lee came home and I woke at the sound of the garage door being raised. The girls came up the stairs eager to see me and then off to watch *Sesame Street* in the back bedroom.

"Something wrong?" Lee asked.

"I'm leaving the shop, Lee."

"When?"

"I guess I should have said I have left the shop. Mr. Krantz let me go today." I told him of the conversation with the shop's owner and I cried while he held me.

"I loved that job," I told him. "I'll never find another one like it."

I let him believe I was heartbroken, when I was really scared. I was ashamed. I was in debt, and now he was, too, only he didn't know it.

I kept the charge accounts secret. I did not tell anyone about them. It was beginning to eat away at the inside of me like a mouse gnawing inside the wall at night.

I put off telling Lee day after day because I thought it might be the end of my marriage. He was so cautious with money—so sensible.

My freedom to spend was gone. My reign of power was

over. I was coming to the end of myself.

After I walked to the mailbox one afternoon, I put my head on the box and surrendered to despair and hopelessness when I took out the dreaded department store monthly billing. There was one the next day, too, and I knew the time had come.

I had to tell Lee what I had done to him . . . to us. And I knew he might leave me.

I waited until that night when we were in bed and he had turned away to go to sleep.

"Lee?"

"Hmm," was the sleepy reply.

"I have something to tell you. . . Please don't turn back over," I paused—"I have done something that I have been putting off telling you and can't any longer."

"Are you all right? Is it the baby?" he asked.

"No. It's not anything to do with the baby and I'm all right. It's just that I have a couple of charge accounts that I haven't told you about and now I can't pay them."

"I thought we agreed that we wouldn't have any charge accounts," he reminded me mildly.

"I know." I really wished at that moment that I had kept my word. "But I do. I can't make the payments since I lost my job."

He was quiet and did not move. "How much do you owe?"

"About $750." I waited for the realization to hit.

There was no response. I lay there in the quiet darkness, with the sound of my own heart beating as loud as a kettle drum in an empty auditorium, and I could hear my blood rushing through my veins, making the same noise as a thunderous waterfall. I felt as though I were dying, but my body wouldn't quit functioning.

Lee didn't move. He simply lay there—still, limp and unresponsive. I didn't sleep all night. I lay there beside my husband, listening to every sound he made in his sleep—

when he finally did sleep. "I probably will never sleep beside him again," I thought. But somewhere in the stillness of the night, the thought invaded my own personal hell that if he stayed with me through this, he would stay with me through anything.

He stayed. He didn't talk much, but he stayed. For the next few weeks we lived in silence. But I was grateful that we were together. I had to give him all the current billings and he took them without comment—all, that is, from the two department stores.

I had not told him about the other two accounts. There was one at a smaller clothing store and one at the shop where I worked. I didn't tell him because I thought that I could manage the payment to the clothing store out of the grocery allowance he gave me each week. I didn't intend to pay the account due the shop. I felt I had it coming since I had not been given any severance or vacation pay.

I was still not ready to assume responsibility for my actions. I went through the whole routine again.

I had to be first to the mailbox.

I had to use part of the grocery money to make the payment.

    The secretiveness,
      The fear,
        The guilt—
          The awfulness of keeping such secrets
            made me a nervous wreck.

I felt that if Lee didn't know the whole truth, I could still preserve some of the knowledge, secretly, about how bad I really was. If he knew how terrible I was, he might still decide to leave me, I reasoned. I did not know what final blow would drive him away, and I did not want to take the chance.

There were payments to make on my car also. And since I couldn't make them and neither could Lee, there was nothing else to do except sell it. It was like losing a piece of myself. That beautiful yellow convertible with the white roof and interior. Remember how all the chrome caught my image and reflected it back to me, as if to say, "Look at who is somebody, driving the snappy car"? I needed that reassurance. But now it would be reflecting someone else's image,

    giving someone else the ego boost,

        making someone else feel important—

        For a while, at least.

One awful day I stood at the bedroom window and watched that someone drive away in my car. Something in the deepest part of me left, too. I said aloud to myself, "Boy! I bet she thinks *she's* something!" But I didn't catch on, even then.

The loss of the car was so depressing, I felt nothing could make things worse.

I might as well tell Lee about the other charge account, I thought. I heard him enter the house through the garage door in the basement. I could hear him doing something in the downstairs closet and finally his footsteps on the stairs. He came down the hall and into our bedroom.

I suppressed the need to cry and he put his arms around me. We stood in silence for a moment. I took a deep breath.

"There's another charge account I haven't told you about," I said bluntly.

"No, Neva! How much longer is this going to go on?" He backed away from me, his face white.

"Is this absolutely all?" Pain and disbelief made his voice crack.

"Yes," I lied. I did not intend to tell him about the one at the shop where I had worked. That was my revenge, not paying it—a rebellious way of striking back at my employer.

"I hope so," he said. He turned and walked out of the bedroom. I knew we wouldn't be speaking for a while again.

Yes, I could remember many things as I stood at my living room picture window that summer's morning, my arms folded over my unborn baby. I wondered what was ahead for me. I wondered if I would ever again feel significant.

"I'll have to become involved in church again," I thought to myself. "If I can just do a few things in my life. . . " Uselessness and discontent had come back as if to stay with me always.

"Where is all the excitement I expected from life? Why isn't it like I wanted it to be? Where has the love gone that I once felt for Lee?" I turned from the window and faced the walls of my home that threatened to be my prison. "Maybe there isn't more to life after all," I told myself. "But will I have to settle for this?" I looked around in despair at the messy house that offered

no challenge,

no solace,

no hope.

Chapter seven

A sudden weight gain in the sixth month of pregnancy alarmed my doctor. I had always had a weight problem, so I wasn't upset. He looked at me over the top of his glasses.

"I don't like this, Neva." He was so serious.

"But I haven't gained even a single pound before this," I defended myself.

"I'm not trying to pick on you. You will have to restrict your diet. Please reduce your salt intake."

"Okay," I promised. And I did, except when I wanted potato chips, or pizza, or spaghetti. I had weighed 195 pounds when I became pregnant. I continued to gain steadily throughout the rest of the pregnancy.

Into the seventh month it was apparent that I had toxemia.

"What does that mean?" I asked.

"It's not good for either you or your baby," the doctor said. It can mean a complicated delivery."

I took the news matter-of-factly with a shrug of my shoulders. God is getting even, I thought.

So, what?
>Will He kill me?
>>I doubt it.
>>>He wants me in better shape than this
>>>>before I die.

"Sit with your legs elevated as much as possible," the doctor instructed. So I sat with my legs up and watched soap operas on TV and learned to crochet while the world went by.

I did the dishes when there were no clean ones left. I washed the clothes when the dresser drawers were empty. I fed the kids when they were hungry. I went to church and wondered, "Why bother?"

Late one afternoon I felt strange sensations across my stomach. I waited for Lee to come home from work.

"I think I might be having contractions," I told Lee. "I timed them—they're eight minutes apart." I didn't feel at all excited.

"We'd better call the doctor." Lee seemed calm enough. I had thought he would be nervous when the time came.

"The doctor says you had better come in," he said after he hung up the phone. "He doesn't want to take any chances since you have had toxemia."

I had packed my suitcase earlier, so it was an easy thing to get ready. We left the girls at a previously arranged home and off we went. The contractions stopped in a few hours and the doctor sent me home the next day.

"Please take it easy and call me if they start up again." He gave me a little hug. "The baby will be coming soon," he encouraged me.

So I went home.

I sat in the recliner chair.

I looked at my elephant legs.

I felt fat, ugly, and worthless.

I went to the doctor the next week for my regular visit and was met with a very surprised reaction.

"I didn't expect to see you here," the doctor said. "I thought that you would call me back and that the baby would have come by now."

I laughed a little laugh that I did not feel inside. "How about it, doctor: is it too late for an abortion?"

"Well, I see you have not lost your sense of humor through all this," he smiled.

"If I still have my sense of humor, it's the only thing I do have left," I said, avoiding his gaze. I was afraid he might realize that my asking for an abortion was not such a joke.

"I want to take some X rays today, Neva. I'm not satisfied with the baby's position.

"I think you ought to know I hate my baby today," I said. I felt no remorse at the admission.

My doctor became my friend that day. He took my hands in his and looked at me. "That's not unusual, Neva. You've been through a lot with this pregnancy, and probably will go through a lot more before it's over." He continued, "You said you hate your baby today; what do you feel other days?"

"Nothing," I said.

It was strange that I felt nothing for my baby. I thought that expectant mothers were to be ecstatic. I was experiencing neutrality in many other areas as well:

my husband,
my daughters,
my parents;
even Jesus.

I had not cried for a long time. Neither had I genuinely laughed. It had been quite awhile since I had experienced any emotion. Inside, I was nothing.

We proceeded with the X rays.

"Do you want to see the pictures, Mrs. Coyle?"

For several years I had gone to this clinic with my children and my husband. I had never seen the X-ray technician in any other mood than this happy-go-lucky one.

"Yeah, sure." I wasn't over-enthusiastic about it.

I looked at the transparency of my huge body, and then she pointed out the outline of my baby.

"Here is his head," she said. "Look here, you can even see his tiny feet, or hers!" She was more excited about my baby than I was. "Look at the tiny spine. Oh, what little hands and arms." I stared at the skeleton of my child.

From the deepest part of my memory some words surfaced, "You did knit me together in my mother's womb. . . . My frame was not hidden from you when I was being formed in secret. . . . Your eyes saw my unformed substance, and in Your book all the days of my life were written, before ever they took shape, when as yet there was none of them" (Ps. 139:13-16).

"My God," it was only a whisper. I clapped my hand to my mouth.

I suddenly felt weak. I sat down. I could not take my eyes from the picture of my baby inside my body. My eyes filled with tears. I choked back a sob.

The technician either ignored or didn't notice my reaction. "I'll take you back to an examining room. The doctor will be with you in a minute."

I stood up. I was more steady now. I looked at the large bulge in my body. I carefully laid my hands on it.

I wasn't empty after all! I carried another human life in there! Suddenly I became aware of another presence inside me that the X ray didn't show. God was there somewhere, and I knew it.

I walked with unsteady steps to the examining room to wait for the doctor.

"Oh, God," I prayed, "I'm sorry for doubting that you have been with me. I'm sorry that I wanted to kill my baby.

"Oh, little person, whoever you are," I cried as I hugged my stomach, "I'm sorry; please forgive your foolish mommy. I'm sorry, baby. I love you." My stomach bulged as the baby moved and kicked. I wept.

"Neva?" the doctor interrupted. "I want to explain something to you." If he noticed the tears, he didn't let on.

"The baby's head is tilted back. We want it tucked, with his little chin resting on his chest. But there is time for all that to happen even in labor. If it doesn't happen, we might consider caesarean section." He looked at me to see how I was taking this latest news.

"It's all right, doctor," I wiped away the tears. I knew that I would have the strength for whatever was ahead for me and my baby. We were not going to go through it alone. God was there. He would take care of everything.

"We'll be all right. I know it."

For the first time, I left the doctor's office excited that I was pregnant. I couldn't wait for Lee to get home.

"Honey," I greeted him at the door, "I saw the baby today! Our baby."

Lee looked at my stomach, and then at my face. "You all right?"

"You should see him, Lee. He's so little. He's upside down. He's got feet, and hands, and a head, and everything!" I shared my excitement of the day with him.

"Is it a boy?" he asked.

"I don't know. I only saw an X ray," I said.

"Oh, an X ray." He was looking at me suspiciously. When he had last seen me just this morning, I had hated being pregnant.

"We're going to have a baby," I announced, as if for the first time.

"I thought so." Lee smiled as he patted my large tummy.

I threw my arms around him and hugged him so tight that I was sure the baby could sense the closeness, too. The baby kicked and we both felt it and laughed together.

"Well, hello in there," I said.

Chapter eight

Early in September, just a week before my due date, I started having contractions again. Once more we made the trip to the hospital. Again the contractions stopped.

"He sure is a stubborn little guy—or girl," the doctor said.

"Do you think it is a boy or a girl?" I asked.

"Yes," was the doctor's reply and I noticed a twinkle in his eye.

I coughed a deep cough that grabbed my chest.

"How long have you had this cough?" he inquired, his brow furrowed.

"Just a few days," I said.

"How do you feel? Besides big, I mean."

"If you want to know the truth," I said, "I feel rotten."

"That's what I thought." He was quiet a minute while he looked over my chart. "How would you feel about staying a few days and let's see if we can get you over whatever bug is plaguing you, okay?"

"It's all right with me," I answered.

"We can't keep you on this floor. This department is reserved for women who are having babies," he teased.

I was moved to a floor for medical patients, and treatment for a bronchial condition lasted almost two weeks. Strict control of my diet and medication during that time brought my toxemia under control.

"How would you like to go home?" the doctor asked one day.

"How would you like to induce labor?" I asked in answer to his question.

"I know it would be nice if it were that simple. But this is not a simple case. Because of the recent toxemia, it would not be a safe thing to do."

"Then I'll go home," I said. "By the way, have you ever had a permanently pregnant patient before?"

The doctor laughed, "Now you sound more like your old self." But I wasn't. I was becoming more and more a new self.

"The baby is pretty small yet, despite your size," he said. I had gained a lot of weight and was about 230 pounds at this point. "Every day you carry the baby is better for him. . . . Be patient, okay?"

"Okay," I promised.

So, overdue, I went home.

More waiting.

More sitting.

But it was different for me now.

Now I was deeply involved with God in assessing my life—

myself,

my purpose,

my worth.

"Please, God, give me some answers to life," I prayed. "Give me some reassurance that there is meaning to all of this."

God let me talk to Him freely.

"I have asked for understanding from those around me, but, God, I received pity. I have asked for acceptance, I have received only tolerance." I was facing God in a new way. I had to admit my faults, confess my sins, and face the truth.

"I've been wrong, Father," I prayed. "I am an independent and willful person. I am selfish and stubborn. Please forgive me—help me to change."

The repentance took weeks. Each time I confessed something to God, He forgave me. It was that simple. Life was beginning for me again with God's forgiveness and help.

With the forgiveness, I was given responsibility:
to know Jesus better,
to study the Bible,
to make things right with Lee.

Through genuine repentance and seeking his forgiveness, too, I had to become the kind of wife he had never had before.

When Lee's forgiveness came, I cried. This time the tears were not of self-pity or depression. They were tears of sorrow. I experienced remorse because of what I had done to him and our girls and myself.

They were also tears of relief and hope. I was experiencing a new beginning with Lee as well as Jesus.

I continued to study and apply myself to learning what God had to say to me in the Bible. I prayed every day, honestly, before God. I admitted all my faults, my shortcomings, biases, frustrations and desires as they happened to me. I was learning to keep my relationship with God current.

As I read the Bible daily, with hunger and desperation, I discovered many passages which mirrored my needs. God began to show me some things I had overlooked in my shallow relationship to Him before.

My concept of Him had been all wrong. He is not
remote,
removed,
and uncaring.
He is
close,
personal,
and concerned.
He is my Father!

He gave me new love. This love flowed out to all the places that were so desperately empty before—my relationship to Him, to Lee, to my children, and to myself.

I could see that even though I had invited Jesus into my heart as a little girl of eleven, I had never given Him complete charge of my life. I had taken things into my own hands. I had been trying to meet my own needs in my own way, in my own strength. I had failed. I wanted God to show me His way. And He did.

I had a need for recognition, and I had turned to people. I was disappointed in the recognition that people give. But He was waiting to give me all the recognition I could possibly use—recognition as His child, a joint heir with His Son Jesus.

I had used my talents and material possessions and my power to gain recognition. God just wanted to shower me with all the benefits of being a child of the King, complete with inheritance.

I had indulged myself in every way by spending money foolishly. I had not the slightest idea of God's plan and purpose for my life.

I had ignored God's will and purpose. I had chosen to obey my fleshly impulses rather than Him.

Rationalization had become a way of life for me. "Everybody likes nice things," I said. "There is no harm in looking nice," I had reasoned. "God wants us to have the best," I had said as I bought expensive clothes I couldn't pay for.

I had used this kind of thinking for getting anything I wanted.

"I can see where I've made many mistakes. O God, can you help me?"

"I can," He said.

"Will I ever get everything straight?" I cried.

"Yes, you will," God answered.

"But, God, I don't understand it all." My mind was in such confusion.

He said, "Lean on, trust and be confident in the Lord with all your heart and mind, and do not rely on your own insight or understanding. In all your ways know, recognize and acknowledge Him, and He will direct and make straight and plain your paths" (Prov. 3:5-6).

"You know, Father, I thought I was so smart."

"Be not wise in your own eyes; reverently fear and worship the Lord, and turn [entirely] away from evil," He said (Prov. 3:7).

I learned that I had to be completely honest before God. "I have this need for things, Father. I give you that need. I know that it is something much deeper. Please show me what it is." I began to learn another type of communication and conversation with God. I asked Him questions out loud. I decided to forget all the old type of prayers I had said before. If God was as real as He seemed to be lately, there was no reason that I could not talk to Him just like I talked to anyone else.

Sometimes God would speak directly to me in my thoughts. Other times He would answer me from the passages in the Bible. It was exciting to discover Him in these new ways.

"About those needs for material things, Neva. Keep out of debt and owe no man anything, except to love one another" (Rom. 13:8). I could see by the instruction in this scripture what I had done in abusing my charge accounts. If God was going to take away the practice of gathering "things" to myself, I knew He was going to meet the need another way. "I have learned how to be content in whatever state I am" (Phil. 4:11). God provided contentment for Paul, and was promising it to me, too.

"What about this self-indulgence in my life, God?"

"I say, walk and live habitually in the (Holy) Spirit—responsive to and controlled and guided by the Spirit; then you will certainly not gratify the cravings and desires of the flesh—of human nature without God" (Gal. 5:16). "The fruit of the Spirit is . . . self-control" (Gal. 5:22-23).

"But God," I said, "what is this 'walking in the Spirit'?"

"In all your ways acknowledge Me and I will direct you"

(Prov. 3:6). He would teach me, in His time.

"There is another area of my life where I see a deep need now. Father, in the name of Jesus, I ask you to minister to me in the vast areas of ignorance." My prayer and desire was to know God and His ways.

"I love those who love me, and those who seek me early and diligently shall find me" (Prov. 8:17). "He who heeds instruction and correction is [not only himself] in the way of life, but is a way of life for others. And he who neglects or refuses reproof [not only himself] goes astray, but causes to err and is a path toward ruin for others" (Prov. 10:17). He would show me.

I read one day, "Do not be vague and thoughtless and foolish, but understanding and firmly grasping what the will of the Lord is" (Eph. 5:17). My immediate reaction was, "Help me, God, to know your will. Give me some guidance in this part of my life today. When I go to bed tonight, I want to know that I walked in your will today."

It seemed that God said, "Great! For openers we'll start with 1 Corinthians 11:3: " 'But I want you to know and realize that Christ is the head of every man, the head of a woman is her husband, and the Head of Christ is God.' "

Because of my helpless state and loss of my income, God had put me in a position of very practical understanding of this principle. I knew that my husband had become boss. He had all the power simply because of my circumstances. He was always to be the head, according to God. But now I was right where God had wanted me all along. "Terrific, God! I understand and receive what you are telling me."

I really wanted to walk in that new knowledge of God's will for my life. I recognized my husband as my head at that moment and have kept him in that position in my heart and practice ever since.

"Now," God said, "what do you suppose your 'head' would like for dinner?" The Lord brings a new dimension to the word "love." When I please Him, He reaches through me to bless others. I went to bed that night ecstatic in the newness of knowing that I had learned a little of God's will and had walked in it. I couldn't wait to find out what He was going to teach me next.

I continued reading scripture for a good part of every day. I was still sitting with my feet elevated many hours at a time. It seemed that God was speaking to me concerning legalism and I wasn't sure what He was trying to say. "I don't understand, God," I would tell Him.

"Be patient," He whispered; "you will."

I read in 2 Corinthians 3:6, "The code of the Law kills, but the Holy Spirit makes alive." And in Philippians 1:9-10, "I pray that your love may abound yet more and more and extend to its fullest development in knowledge and all keen insight—that is, that your love may [display itself in] greater depth of acquaintance and more comprehensive discernment; so that you may surely learn to sense what is vital, and approve and prize what is excellent and of real value—recognizing the highest and the best, and distinguishing the moral differences; and that you may be untainted and pure and unerring and blameless, that—with hearts sincere and certain and unsullied—you may approach the day of Christ, not stumbling nor causing others to stumble."

God was preparing me for the freedom of the walk in the Spirit.

Sometimes I became discouraged.

"Lord, I don't feel I can make it today. I try so hard and just foul everything up. I yell at the kids. I am impatient with Lee. Help me, God."

"Just let go, Neva. I'll help you," He said.

"Thank you, Father. You just saved my life again."

"He who began a good work in you will continue until the day of Jesus Christ—right up to the time of His return—developing [that good work] and perfecting and bringing it to full completion in you" (Phil. 1:6). I could see that even though I was tempted to give up on myself, God was not. He had made an investment in me, His Son. He was going to see this thing through. And with His help, so would I.

There were times of discouragement when I felt I would never get things right in my mind and in my life. I was right. I never would. God would. My needs were great, but I found Him to be so much greater and better equipped than I was. I learned to pray: "Help me, Lord. Teach me, Father. When I try it on my own I ruin things and make huge messes. With you I can do anything."

God said,

    "I've just been waiting to hear you say that.

        I'll take over from here,"

           And He did.

             He's my Father.

My full inheritance as His daughter was about to start unfolding for me and for my family.

I learned about the husband-wife relationship, and how it is compared in the Scripture to our relationship to Christ and the church. Wow! That was new to me!

In the fifth chapter of the book of Ephesians, it talks along these lines: "I speak to you concerning the mystery of Christ and His church." Here I found lots of food for thought. I imagined the ideal situation of a church depending, actively and purposefully, on Christ for everything (Eph. 5:24). I thought I would begin to treat my husband in the same manner. The result was beautiful. In verse 29, I realized that my husband was instructed to nourish, carefully protect and cherish me—taking care of all my basic needs. I saw that that could leave me a lot of room to grow in an atmosphere free from worry. I read in the 22nd verse that I was to submit to my husband. I was willing to try it.

I imagined the ideal church taking every decision to Jesus for consideration and asking His guidance in every area. I practiced this principle on my husband with great anticipation, and I have not been disappointed.

I have found for myself, by deliberate practice and experimentation, that everything which applies to my relationship with Christ can be applied with outstanding results to my relationship with my husband. My love must grow

for Christ,
     for my husband.
I had to look for ways to know
     the Lord,
          and Lee.
I must submit
     to the Lord,
          and to my husband.
I couldn't ever again allow anything to come
     between God and me,
          or Lee and me.

Once I got that part of my life straightened out, it was really time for our baby to be born.

"You okay, honey?" Lee asked.

"I just have to go to the bathroom," I said. I got out of bed in the dark and turned on the hall light.

"What time is it?" I could tell Lee was not asleep but not awake either.

"About midnight or thereabouts," I said over my shoulder.

"Praise God, it won't be long now," I whispered as I went back to bed.

"Can we get some sleep now?" Lee said.

"Um-mm." I closed my eyes again.

"Lee!" I was suddenly wide awake.

"Oh, no," Lee grumbled.

"My water broke!" I said.

"I'd better call the doctor."

"I'll get the kids up," I said and got up and headed for the girls' room.

"I called the doctor. He thinks you ought to go to the hospital." He looked funny half dressed. "I called your mom, too. She'll take the girls."

"I feel a contraction," I whispered. I didn't want to upset the girls. I had never had a pain give me so much excitement before! I giggled.

In the car the contractions increased. I shivered in the coldness of the November night. When we arrived at my mother's house, she came out to the car to help carry in the girls.

"Don't worry about anything, honey," she said. "We'll manage. Just have the baby, okay?"

"I'll sure try, Mom." I kissed her.

"Well, Mrs. Coyle. Going to try again?" The nurse in the emergency entrance of the hospital recognized us.

"I thought I might," I teased back.

I was wheeled to the labor room and settled in as much as possible.

"Mr. Coyle, you're shivering," a nurse observed.

"I can't seem to get warm," he said.

The nurses covered him with blankets and gave him as much encouragement as they could.

I was in labor all night.

"You are just not dilating, Mrs. Coyle. It will be quite awhile." The nurse turned to Lee, "Why don't you go on home, and we'll call you in plenty of time."

"Do you mind, sweetie?" He looked so tired.

"Go ahead, Lee. I'll be all right."

He kissed me and left. I wanted to cry, but instead I prayed. I couldn't get comfortable. I lay on my back. I lay on my side. It didn't seem to make any difference. Twelve hours passed and I still had not dilated to more than five centimeters. The doctor told me that they would be considering caesarean section. He called in a surgeon.

"Let's let her go a while longer," the surgeon said.

"Oh, brother, I want this over with," I told my nurse.

I began hard labor at that point. Each contraction felt

as if I were being thrust out the bottom of the bed.

"Okay," the cheery surgeon said as he entered the labor room.

"What's happening?" I demanded between contractions, which were now almost constant.

"Your baby's decided to come the regular way after all," he said.

"When?" I asked.

"Any day now," my nurse, Earline, laughed.

"Very funny!"

"Call her husband and tell him to hurry."

"I did," another nurse said. "He'll be here any minute."

"What's she doing?" I heard my husband's voice.

"She's hard at work," the nurse said.

"You okay, honey?" he asked from a safe distance.

"She can't talk now. We're going into delivery," the nurse told him.

I went into the delivery room and met my doctor who had come on the run.

"How are you doing?" he asked.

"Great, I think." I was so excited I could hardly concentrate on the job at hand.

"It's a boy!"

I heard the suction and then the sharp cry of my baby, my son!

"A boy!" It was Lee's voice. He stood looking in the window of the delivery room.

I began to laugh and cry at the same time.

"I want to see him. Is he all right? Is he normal? Is he okay? Can I hold him?"

"Hey, slow down, girl." The doctor was standing by my side. "He looks real good." Was that a tear in the eye of my big strong doctor?

The nurse held out my son and I took him in my arms, close to me, and they wheeled me and baby back into the labor room.

I presented to my husband our son, Dan Ryan.

"Here he is, Lee. Isn't he something?"

"Look at that, a boy." Lee seemed stunned.

We spent some time together just looking at our son and then Lee gave me a kiss and said, "I love you."

Chapter nine

The next few months I kept on with my search in the Scriptures and took care of my little family. I learned that when you honestly and openly seek God, He reveals himself in places you'd never expect, with impact you'd never imagine.

I had spent much time in struggling to know God better. I had sought God many times at the altar in our church following services for ministry. Every time I left such a session in which I had poured out my heart and soul to God, completely spending myself emotionally as I sobbed and cried out to God, I thought, "Surely it will work now."

But it didn't.

"Living for Jesus will be easier now."

But it wasn't.

"Take it by faith," I had been told.

"Walk in the Spirit," I was directed.

"Only believe," I was exhorted.

One day after I had had one of these sessions with God, I lost my temper and became angry with someone. "Wait a minute," I argued. Hadn't I already crucified the old man? How could I become angry? If the "old man" is dead, who resurrected him in me, and how many times will he have to die in order to *stay* dead?

I was ready to give up in despair until I rationalized that I could go ahead and *feel* angry but merely *act* as if I were not. I could suppress it. Who would ever know?

I didn't feel very holy, but I had learned to look holy. I could sound holy, and I knew the vocabulary in order to pray holy.

I had memorized a list of religious do's and don't's and was living by that. Do attend church, pray aloud, sing, give testimonies; don't holler at the kids (in public), don't be extravagant, in dress, don't upset my husband. . . . I could not be bothered with letting God reveal to me *His* way of living a holy life.

I had learned to be a legalist. It was so much easier than letting God get ahold of the real me, the one inside which no one could see—except my husband and children when I momentarily lost control in a particularly stressful situation. I was a spiritual cripple, limping along as best I could, fairly satisfied with the status quo until someone or something "ticked me off." Then I had doubts and moments of wondering if there were not a better way.

To compensate for these moments, I reasoned that our church had the truth of God—we members were "true Christians." And I looked "down my spiritual nose" at other denominations in order to feel better about myself.

One day a friend called. "Hello, Neva. I thought I would call and invite you and Lee to dinner next week." It was fun to hear her voice. "Well, you know, we always say we are going to eat together more than once a year," she continued; "and I thought I would do something about all of our good intentions."

"Sounds great, but let me check with Lee and I'll get back to you tomorrow." I wanted to go, even though they had left our denomination, and I felt it would be all right with Lee, too.

"We have invited some other friends, too," she said when I called to accept the next day. "We know you and Lee will like them; they are really special people."

The prearranged evening arrived, and after introductions we started the routine of becoming acquainted.

Wow! These people knew and loved Jesus in a way that attracted me like a magnet. They praised the Lord out loud during table grace. They praised the Lord during the dinner conversation.

"Where did you say you go to church?" Lee asked as we ate:

"St. Peter's Catholic Parish," they answered.

My dessert got caught in my throat, and I reached for a glass of water. Catholic! They were *Catholic*!

How could these Catholics be so enthusiastic about Jesus? I mean, they sounded positively *evangelical*! It couldn't be so, but it was. I listened with great interest as these "Catholic Christians" talked about Jesus, how He was involved in their daily lives and the lives of their children. I also noticed that our hosts had a deep, serious enthusiasm for their relationship with Jesus. "A little strange, even for evangelicals," I thought. What do they know about Jesus that I could have possibly missed? I was such a "good" Christian!

Lee and I just looked at each other. When we got in the car later, Lee said, "They really have something, don't they?"

"But, Lee, they are Catholics!" I said, letting my biases show.

"I know," he said. I knew what my husband was thinking.

"But they're such beautiful Christians. How can they be *Catholic*?" I verbalized our confusion.

God also heard that question and began to bring me into contact with warm, radiant believers from even "mainline" denominations which I had considered to be "dead." I wanted what they had!

I began to plot:

"Why don't we go to church with your mother next Sunday, honey?" I asked Lee later the next week.

"What?" Lee looked shocked.

"Well, it is Mother's Day, and no one should object if we went with her." We were still very concerned with what the other people in our church thought and said. "Nobody would care if she came and visited with us, would they?"

"Well, no." I could tell he was thinking it over.

I had reasons other than Mother's Day for wanting to attend that church. It happened to be the same church where our friends who had hosted the dinner attended. I was very curious, also a little scared.

We entered the church from the back and had to walk down a hall which passed the junior department of the Sunday school. Our friend was a teacher in there and he spotted us. He crossed the room and met us in the hall.

"Well, look who is here!" I knew he would be surprised, but I was not prepared for his next remark. "Praise the Lord!" This guy praises the Lord for everything, I thought. I wonder if he's serious. (I found out later that he does seriously praise God all the time.)

It was like coming in out of a cold storm and being greeted by a friend who knew you were coming and who had warmed a quilt to wrap around you. So comfortable, warm and restful. We knew we would return, and we did.

I was still a little cautious; I mean, this church was very different from ours, and I was not quite ready to let go of my spiritual snobbishness.

But I felt the warmth,
    the love,
        and the comfort
            I had needed for a good, long time.

I had many questions about the new insights we were having in the sermons and Bible studies. People whom I knew in our other church would call me up and warn me about many things they had heard about this other group, and I learned just to funnel all the questions and doubts to Jesus.

"It's only an emotional trip," I was told. I asked Jesus about it one night in a service where people were praising God. He said to me, "See how calm the people are?" And they were. Just beautiful, and peaceful, too.

"Speaking in tongues is from the devil," I was warned.

"And everyone present was filled with the Holy Spirit

and began speaking in languages they didn't know, for the Holy Spirit gave them this ability" (Acts 2:4, TLB).

"That doesn't sound to me like it comes from the devil," I said.

"But the gifts of the Spirit were for apostolic times; this is today and we don't need all that stuff," another friend said and for proof quoted 1 Corinthians 13:8, TLB: "All the special gifts and powers from God will some day come to an end, but love goes on forever. Some day prophecy, and speaking in unknown languages, and special knowledge—the gifts will disappear." However, I had heard speaking in tongues for myself, and the interpretation was such a blessing and encouragement to me to keep on searching for God in His fullness. My own experience denied that the need for spiritual gifts was passed.

As I read on in this passage, it only further proved to me that I was getting closer to knowing that the time for gifts has indeed not disappeared. "Now we know so little, even with our special gifts, and the preaching of those most gifted is still so poor. But when we have been made perfect and complete, then the need for these inadequate special gifts will come to an end, and they will disappear" (1 Cor. 13:9-10, TLB). I, for one, had not yet been made perfect and complete. I had not heard any perfect preaching. Therefore, according to this verse, I knew that I and many more like me needed the spiritual gifts more than ever. My friend became very discouraged at this time and gave up this approach only to try another.

"All you want," she continued, "is special proof that you have been 'sanctified,' and you shouldn't seek God for a sign. He didn't give it to me and He won't give it to you. If He wanted me to speak in tongues, He would just give it to me. I wouldn't have to go asking for it."

"That's the whole point," I said. "I'm not going to ask God for tongues. I'm going to ask Him to fill me with the Holy Spirit."

"Well, that's a relief," she responded.

"But, you know, the more questions you ask me, the more I search the Bible for answers and the more I see clearly that being filled with the Holy Spirit means involvement with spiritual gifts." I really could see the possibilities for me.

"Oh, brother, I give up!" she said, and hasn't asked me another question since.

I had lived about eighteen years as a Christian without any power for witnessing or power to live above temptation and circumstances in my life, and I didn't want to go on any longer in that condition. "You shall receive power when the Holy Spirit has come upon you; and you shall be my witnesses. . ." (Acts 1:8)—that was what I wanted.

For a while we attended our old church on Sunday mornings and my mother-in-law's church on Sunday evenings. However, we felt as if those precious Sunday evening services were stolen, and we knew we couldn't continue this arrangement on a permanent basis. Lee and I began to check out with the Bible everything we heard in the sermons. And after a while our only reply to questioning friends was, "It's in the Bible," or "It's scriptural." Such a simple answer. But God is not complicated. We finally, following much thought and prayer, changed churches at the end of the summer of 1972.

In one particular Sunday evening service, I heard an evangelist preach on the topic: "One Greater Than Solomon Is Here." The presence of Jesus was so real to me. My heart pounded as the speaker invited those who desired the reality of Jesus in their lives to come forward.

I hesitated only slightly and then stepped out into the aisle. I wished at that moment that I had selected a seat closer to the front. The walk down the aisle seemed a mile long.

Kneeling at the altar that night I found Jesus in a new way—as Baptizer in the Holy Spirit. Having gone to the service alone, I was anxious to return home and share with Lee.

I walked into the house and sensed that all was quiet. I hoped the baby would stay sleeping so I could tell Lee, without interruption, what had happened to me.

"Lee?" I didn't turn on the bedroom light.

"That you?" he said from under the covers.

"Honey, I was filled with the Holy Spirit tonight."

"You what?" He quickly came out from under the blanket and, propped up on one elbow, stared at me.

"They gave an invitation and I went forward. Someone prayed with me and I received the Holy Spirit."

"That's great!" And he genuinely meant it.

Submerged in the presence of Jesus, that night I slept like a baby. I was one of God's born-again children and now I had been baptized in His Spirit as well. He would teach me anything and everything I needed to know as long as I stayed close to Him.

The next thing He taught me was how to forgive.

There had been a friend in my life for quite a while whose relationship with me had, at best, its ups and downs. She had done something that hurt me deeply. The next day after receiving the baptism in the Holy Spirit, I felt drawn to pray for her. It seemed strange at the time, for she attended our old church and I wanted to put all of the memories there far behind me. But I went to my room when the children took their naps and Rhonda was in afternoon kindergarten. I knelt beside my bed. "Father," I began, "I want to talk to you about Lynn." (I'm using a different name.) "It is clear to me that the relationship I have had with her is not pleasing to her, to me, or to you. I have been hurt deeply by some of the things she has done and said. I know I have not always been what she has needed in a friend, either. God, I want to ask you to forgive me, and I want to forgive her; and God, I want to ask you to forgive her, too."

I was quiet for a minute or two. "I can't think of anything else to say, but I don't feel as if this closes the issue." Another minute of silence. "God, you know if it has all been prayed or not. If this prayer is to go on, you'll have to pray it through me." I paused.

Then, without any effort on my part—cooperation, yes, for the voice was mine, but effort, no—I began to pray in another language—a language I had never even heard before, much less learned.

The Spirit of God swept over me, cleansing me from bitter feelings, unforgiveness and jealousy. When I was done, I was clean, refreshed, calm, and filled with love for someone whom I had come close to hating.

Shortly after this experience, my husband and I attended a seminar designed for growing Christians, and I found that I had others to forgive as well. I also discovered through the scriptural teaching at the seminar that there were some people whom I had to ask to forgive me for hurting or offending them in some way in the past. I found that God prepared the way for me in every instance, and not one person refused my request for forgiveness.

There was an old boyfriend in high school whom I had wronged in our dating relationship by self-centered attitudes. God arranged a meeting with him when I went back to California for a visit to my grandmother. He accepted the Lord then and is a vital Christian today.

I had to ask my employer to forgive me for my attitude those last days of working. Because he is a busy executive working in Arizona, I wrote him a letter.

"Dear Mr. Krantz," I said. "God has been dealing with me concerning some bad attitudes in my life. When I left your employment, I owed the shop $55.00 in a personal charge account, and I refused to pay it, as you know. I want to ask you to allow me to owe you this amount as an honest debt and would ask you to forgive me for the wrong I have done you." He wrote me a beautiful letter.

"Dear Neva," he wrote in his own handwriting, "Thank you for your thoughtful letter. Please be assured I have always had great respect for you. You worked very hard, and the $55.00 was repaid to me many times in your devotion to duty. Please consider it canceled. B. Krantz."

I was learning what it was to experience forgiveness and to receive it openly.

My husband forgave me.

God forgave me.

But most surprising of all, I learned that
I had to forgive myself.

Whereas in days gone by I had experienced depression and nothingness, now I was filled with hope every waking hour of the day. I had physical strength like I had never experienced before. My energy level was at an all-time high. I could see good changes in my life. There was freshness in my marriage. I was experiencing stability in other important relationships as well.

Everything was going well—everything except one thing. I was steadily gaining weight. I had weighed 240 pounds when Danny was born, and now I was up another five pounds.

"What am I going to do now?" I wondered.

Chapter ten

God began to deal with me concerning how I felt about myself. He used His Word along with the witness within my spirit. One day the scale read 248 pounds! I was very uncomfortable about how I looked to others, especially to my husband.

My clothes didn't fit anymore. All those beautiful clothes that I "had" to possess when I was working just hung there in my closet, mocking me. I had only one dress I could wear to church and a large black coat that I never took off in public. I avoided looking at my reflection in store windows when I went grocery shopping. I removed the mirror on our dresser. I sat near the back seat in church. Whenever I could not avoid having my picture taken, I "hid" behind one of my children. (Have you ever seen an elephant hide behind a rabbit?) I found myself eating constantly when alone, but almost nothing at mealtimes.

"I don't understand it," Lee had said. "How can you be gaining weight when you eat like a bird?"

I had heard about an operation that causes obese people to lose weight very rapidly, and thought right away, "That's for me." I began asking questions of former patients who had had it done, and became convinced it was the answer to all my problems which were "weighing" me down. I would feel better about myself, and then God wouldn't get after me for feeling so inferior anymore.

If I were slim and skinny
    I wouldn't be inferior anymore—
        so I thought.

I made the necessary appointment to see the surgeon who was performing bypass surgeries, but before I went to him I saw Dr. Summers, my own family doctor.

"I've made an appointment to see Dr. John," I told him.

"Really? What for?" he asked.

"I want to have a bypass. Do you know Dr. John? What do you know about the bypass?" I said.

"Yes, I know Dr. John." I knew he did. "I'm not sure that he'll do it on you, though."

"Why not?" I asked.

"You are not big enough, Neva." He leaned back in his chair. "This operation is only for hopelessly obese people."

I looked at the floor. "That's me, hopelessly obese," I said.

"You have gained up to the weight you were when Danny came, haven't you?"

"Yes." It was a hard admission for me to make to anyone.

"Well, go see him then, but I hope you won't be too disappointed if he doesn't accept you as a patient." He was kind to warn me.

"If he does, will you come and see me in the hospital?" I said.

"Sure, I'll be in to see you."

I wanted to tell him how much his support meant to me. He hadn't laughed at me. I had first come to this office as a frightened teen-ager, uncertain about life and what it held for me. He had encouraged me then and again when my relationship with Lee had been so unsure. I had brought daughters as newly adopted infants for his inspection and subsequent approval. He had taken care of me through my pregnancy. He had watched me change and encouraged me in ways that were overt as well as covert. I had come to love this great man as much as any patient ever loved and respected a doctor. It seemed that there was not a good way to tell him, and so my gratitude hung there in the room unsaid and unexpressed.

The day finally arrived for my appointment with Dr. John. I drove in to town and parked the car in the parking lot by the Medical Arts Building. It was the fall of the year and the air was crisp and clear. As I approached the entrance to the tall building I paused. "What if this isn't God's will?" I shoved the thought aside. I waited for the elevator after consulting the building directory. "If I wasn't so fat I could walk the four flights," I thought. The elevator door opened and I put away any thought of climbing the stairs.

"What if this isn't God's will?" The nagging thought persisted.

"Four!" I said aloud. "This is my floor. Excuse me, please."

As I approached the office door, again the thought came, "What if this isn't God's will?" I slowed my pace and considered the thought.

"If it isn't God's will, I won't do it." That seemed simple enough. I got a drink of water from the fountain. "But how will I know?"

"Oh, boy," I thought. "I'd better have a plan by which I can determine whether or not this is God's will."

I decided I would take any negative response from the receptionist as a "no" from God.

I surely put a lot of responsibility on that poor receptionist, and she did not even know it. I set my purse on the counter to fill out the required forms.

"Say, that is a nice purse. I have wanted one like it for myself." It was a basket purse with a hand-painted top and a wooden cut-out scene. I had made it and many others like it, and had been selling them for a long time.

"I saw some like this at an art fair this past summer," she continued. "I sure wanted to buy one, but I didn't, and I've been sorry ever since."

I began to fill out the forms she handed me.

"How do you like it?" she asked.

"Like what?" I replied.

"The purse. I am really struck with it."

"I like it fine," I said. I handed her the filled-out form.

"Are you 'Neva'?" She looked at the form.

"Yes," I said, "I am. Why do you ask?"

"The name on the purse is 'Neva.' Did you make it?"

"Yes, I did."

"It's really beautiful." She smiled at me.

"Thank you." I returned her smile. I thought, "This is God's way of telling me that the operation is all right with Him."

If it was all right, then why did I feel such a hesitancy? I had not learned at this time about following the witness in my spirit. The surgeon was such a nice, warm doctor, and I liked and trusted him immediately. Many of the uncertain feelings faded for the moment.

Everyone who is a candidate for this type of surgery has to have a psychiatric exam, and I was no exception. Sometimes people are hiding very severe psychological problems under tons of fat; and when the fat problem is removed, they are left with all their problems exposed and they can't handle it. If psychiatric problems turn up in the exam, the patient is treated for them first, sometimes solving the overweight crisis through therapy and counseling rather than surgery.

It was, for the most part, a pleasant, interesting experience. The written exams were sort of a drag, and I began to feel a little paranoid because of the many different ways that the same questions were asked. I knew that I would probably be labeled a religious fanatic because I stated that I knew God saw everything I did and knew everything I thought and heard every word I said. I thought that this would be okay if a Christian scored the results, but since I was filling out the kind of paper that is scored by a machine, I was sure I was sunk.

My interview with the psychiatrist was most surprising, in that I found myself relaxed and comfortable, sharing some of the most intimate parts of myself that I had not shared with anyone before; and he was positive and encouraging in his responses to me. He picked up the phone and dialed a number.

"Dr. John please, Dr. Janisch calling." He looked at me. "Dr. John, Neva is here with me now. I haven't scored her tests yet, but I'm sure I can give you a go-ahead from my office right now."

He smiled at me. "Oh, yeah? I'll ask her." He covered the mouthpiece of the phone with his hand. "Dr. John says he has time to see you right now if you want to stop down at his office and set up the surgery date."

"Is he here in this building today?" Dr. John had two offices and I was downtown in the Medical Arts Building that day.

"Yes," he said.

"Well, sure, if he has the time. I'd really like to get things moving." There was a lump in my stomach.

"She'll be right down, Dr. John," he said back into the phone. After he hung up and I put on my coat, he opened the door for me and said, "Good luck, Neva."

"Thank you," I said, "I'll need it!"

My heart pounded as I entered the door of the other office. "I'm just excited," I tried to rationalize. "Everybody is nervous at the prospect of surgery." I thought of the other women I had seen who had had this surgery and how slim and trim most of them looked. "And they started out even bigger than I am."

I ignored the ones with flabby skin so loose that they had to have additional surgery to remove the excess flesh and skin. I ignored the patients who had suffered with electrolyte imbalance and had to be hospitalized with intravenous feedings. I ignored the ones who had severe psychological problems. None of that would happen to me. I had God.

I introduced myself to the receptionist and she was very

crisp and businesslike. "Yes, the doctor is expecting you. Come right in," she said.

"Well, Neva, Dr. Janisch says you're all right. If you say you're all right and if you agree, we'll arrange your surgery date. What sounds good for you?"

"Right after the 5th of January, if it is okay," I said. "That looks fine to me. I'll be going out of town for a little vacation on the 10th. The 9th is open—is that okay?"

"Okay with me," I said.

Arrangements were made for the care of my children. A young student nurse named Marilyn had volunteered to stay with us for the duration of my hospitalization and through the next couple of weeks to see that I was all right. Looking back now, I know that I never could have gone through what I did if it had not been for her help. She had a quarter off from school for independent study, so we arranged the surgery date around that.

Upon admittance to the hospital, questions were asked about every part of my life. My medical history was examined, my eating habits explored, my feelings about the surgery were brought into the open. I was asked questions about my plans for the future, about my children, and my husband. With each question I grew more and more

anxious,

nervous,

scared,

and doubtful.

How do you know God's will? I wondered.

The next morning my surgery was scheduled for 8:00, and at 7:00 I was given a hypo that sent me into a twilight state. My mother referred to it as an "I don't care shot," but it wasn't for me.

I did care.

I still had fear gnawing at my rib cage.

I was terrified.

I was screaming inside.

The pastor and his wife, my parents, and my husband came, and we had prayer together. Or at least they had prayer together. The only thing I could concentrate on was the time, and 8:00 was just ten minutes away. I would be put to sleep then and the screaming within me would be stilled and I would rest.

Eight o'clock came, and I remember thinking, "They will have to come for me soon or I will be late, and the doctor might not do it for me because I am late." I had a mental picture of him standing by the table, scalpel in hand, looking at his watch and saying, "I'll give her only a few more minutes and then I'm leaving."

"Mrs. Coyle, are you sleeping?" the nurse had come over and touched my hand.

"Not quite," I said.

"The doctor called up from surgery and said it will be delayed a little while. He has an emergency he had to take care of."

She left the room. I started to cry.

An emergency! I remember thinking that if he knew what was going on in my head, he would realize that he had another emergency already in progress. The hour's delay seemed like an eternity, and my fear and anxiety turned to panic and agony.

My father and the pastor, both being congenial men, passed the hour very quickly with light conversation I couldn't understand, mingled with occasional laughter that seemed to me like someone laughing inside of an empty barrel. My mother and the pastor's wife visited together and tried, at times, to include me in their conversation. I joined in as best I could, but I could not make myself be heard. All this time my husband kept his hand on my head. He did not talk. The concern I felt from his touch was almost more than I could bear, but I could not let him go away from me either. He needed to touch me as much as I needed the reassurance of his presence and his love.

Finally it was time to go. The surgical cart came and still I wanted someone to forbid me to go through with it. But no one did.

The cart was narrow, hard and cold. The ride to surgery was too long, too bumpy, and over with too soon.

Dr. John came into surgery and spoke to me.

"Well, Neva. How are you doing? A little scared maybe? You will be going to sleep soon."

He held my hand for a minute. I wanted to ask him to pray, but I didn't know how he would respond. I couldn't bear it if he refused. So I didn't ask.

"I'm doing fine," I lied instead. "Dr. John?" I said, wanting to tell him how much I appreciated what he was about to do for me. I couldn't find the right words under the influence of the drugs given to me before. "I'm going to be all right, I know it." But I really didn't.

"Ready to go to sleep now?" someone at my head asked.

I nodded my head in the affirmative and held tightly to Dr. John's hand. With the stabbing sensation of the needle in my vein, I drifted into blackness, peace, only to awaken immediately with the room spinning.

I was still screaming inside: "Tell the doctor to stop, I'm not asleep after all!" I couldn't seem to make anyone hear me. "I am awake," I tried again. "I am choking!" I called out. There was a stabbing pain in my stomach. "Tell the doctor to stop. I can feel pain!" I was trying to pull out whatever was choking me.

"Mrs. Coyle!" a voice said. "Neva! You're all right. It's all over with. Please relax; you're doing fine."

"Doing fine!" I tried to say. "I'm choking to death."

I drifted back into blackness. I learned later that I had been trying to pull out the tube that was put down my throat into my stomach for the surgery. When I woke up again the tube was gone and so was the choking sensation.

I saw the doctor later that night, after I was back in my own room, and I wanted to tell him how grateful I was for this chance to be slim, but I was so groggy that I couldn't make much sense. My husband stayed by my side for a while. It seemed as if he were there constantly, but each time he spoke to me he was wearing a different shirt. I puzzled at this until he told me that he was in and out for a day or so, and the only time I woke up was when he spoke to me.

When I did finally wake up completely, it was to pain, both in my stomach and in my arm, where I was receiving intravenous feeding. Ordinarily IV's don't hurt, but when there is the combination of small veins and IV's loaded with vitamins and potassium, they do.

"Nurse," I cried when she responded to my call, "this hurts so bad I can't take it!"

"You have to, Neva. I know they're painful, but it's essential for you to keep your chemical balance."

"Does it have to go in so fast?"

"If we are to keep on schedule it does."

"Is the schedule more important than me?" I was in intense pain.

"Well, I'll slow it down just a bit. How's that?"

"Better—not much, but some," I said.

The flow was eventually turned down so low that it took up to twelve hours for a six-hour dose. I would just get one nurse convinced that it hurt as much as it did, and she would go off duty and another nurse would come, check it, and turn it up again—and I would have to go through the process all over again.

"Oh, God," I cried, "is this intense pain part of the punishment for being so fat?"

One night at the eleven-o'clock-shift change, a nurse poked her head into my room. "You still awake, Neva?" It was a cute little lady who was planning on retiring in a year or two.

"Yes, I can't get to sleep. The IV's hurt too much." I started to cry. They had been in place for five days.

"Let me have a look." She started toward my bed.

"Promise me you won't turn it up," I begged.

"Okay," she said after her inspection; "it really looks sore. There are red streaks all the way to your elbow. Boy, it's really swollen, isn't it? Let's put a cold pack on it."

I felt some relief with the cold compress. I fell into a light sleep. I woke with someone standing quietly by my bed.

"Oh, hi," I said, recognizing the same nurse.

"I didn't mean to wake you up. I just wanted to check that arm," she said.

She switched on the overhead light and looked at my arm.

"Oh, bother," she said.

"What's the matter?"

"The vein has collapsed," she said. "I'll have to call someone to start it again. I'll be right back."

She left my room. I fell apart.

She poked her head back into the doorway in just a few seconds.

"Neva? I just thought of something." She slowly came to my side. "Do you believe in prayer?"

"Boy, I sure do," I said wiping the tears away.

"Well, I'm going to call the doctor, but I thought that you should be praying while I make the call."

"All right," I agreed.

She left my room again and I began to pray. Wow! Did I ever pray!

A few minutes passed and she popped in with, "Praise the Lord! We're taking them out!"

"For how long?" I felt a glimmer of hope.

"For good. Dr. John gave an order to discontinue."

"Dr. John?" I was surprised. "I thought he was on vacation."

"Well, he just got back today," she smiled. "Just in time."

A Holy-Spirit-directed nurse had discerned that God

was saying I had had enough and my body was rejecting the medication. The swelling in my arm was present for several more days, but the pain and burning fever left immediately and I was able to sleep.

This was my first experience with a nurse who knew the power of prayer and wanted to pass it on to me.

The next day another nurse, not on staff but a visitor, came to me. She was a member of our new church.

"Neva, dear, I have been observing you," she said. I gave her my full attention. She was one of the older women in our congregation. Her white hair fell into place in perfect harmony with her lovely countenance. "Yes, I believe God has some special plans for you."

"He does? Me?"

"Yes, Neva, you. But there is something very important you must learn. It is essential to your own spiritual well-being and equally important to your emotional well-being."

She leaned closer to me as if to reveal some highly classified secret. Her eyes radiated the love of Jesus Christ. I sensed Him closer than I had since coming into the hospital. I couldn't wait to hear this very important thing she was about to tell me.

"It's time you learned to praise the Lord," she said.

"I do know how," I said.

"Not by the looks of things here." She looked seriously at me. "Praise is the most effective tool you have available to you to get through times like this. It is a serious weapon you have right here within yourself. It's time you learned to praise God in the tough situations as well as in church services where it is easy."

I knew just by looking at her that she was concerned and intent on teaching me this new spiritual insight. I was about to learn to praise God in adversity, like it or not.

"Well," she said, "let's get on with it."

I knew that there was no arguing with this lovely, soft-spoken ambassador of Jesus. I began to praise the Lord in my new prayer language, and she encouraged me with every syllable. My attitude and outlook started to change. I became more joyous with every moment I praised the Lord.

"Now," she said, "you will begin to get well." I hugged her with grateful tears streaming down my face.

"Don't you stop when I leave, either," she warned. I knew I didn't dare. So I kept on. I learned the power of praise just in time. The next few months were very hard on my family and me.

The first month after surgery I lost only eighteen pounds; and I was very disappointed, after hearing reports of others losing thirty-five to forty pounds in the same amount of time.

"I don't want you to be discouraged," Dr. John said. "Each patient is different. Just give it time."

There had been a period after surgery when I was not permitted to swallow anything for five days. I thought that if I had done that on my own, I could have lost eighteen pounds without the surgery.

I was learning to practice praising God in everything.

There were many days in the next few months that I could not even get out of bed. My pre-surgery doubts came flooding back, and I began to think that I had made a terrible mistake in having surgery. Not feeling well, I also was beginning to be ridden with guilt as well. I was sure that God was not letting me lose weight as fast as I had hoped for one reason—He was mad at me. And now I was feeling
    fat
        inferior,
           and, in addition to that,
              guilty.

I thought that my surgery was supposed to take care of all my inferiority problems, but instead it had just added the unbearable burden of guilt and condemnation as well.

It took many months before I began to feel even a semblance of good health. Then I was again looking for projects to do "for the Lord" to satisfy my need for acceptance.

Since we had changed churches after my experience of receiving the power of the Holy Spirit, I hadn't been involved in church work at all.

My pastor had approached me about this once while visiting me in the hospital. "Neva," he said, "when you are better I want you to pray about what the Lord would have you do at church."

"What do you mean, Pastor Ken?" *Pray about* what the Lord would have me do? That was a switch! Previously I had done what the *pastor* had thought the Lord would have me do.

"I have found out, in my experience, that only what has the calling of God on it also has His anointing," he explained. "There is no time for Christian busy-work. God knows the needs of a church and He knows the people who attend there. He knows who can do what. If we all listened to the call of God and obeyed Him, there would not be any job left undone in the church. That is why I urge you to pray as to what the Lord would have you do. I'm sure the responsibility He calls you to will fit a need the church has as well."

This was a new way of looking at church work. I had never asked the Lord what He wanted from me in connection with my church work before. I had gotten as busy as possible and hoped that somehow I would fit His will.

"All our efforts," Pastor continued, "are of the greatest value to God and to us when they are in direct obedience to Him."

Many times since, this teaching has helped me to keep any project that I might be working on in proper perspective.

I saw later a verse, Ephesians 2:10 in The Amplified Bible, that said the same thing: "Now we are God's [own] handiwork (His workmanship), recreated in Christ Jesus, [born anew] that we may do those good works which God predestined (planned beforehand) for us, (taking paths which He prepared ahead of time) that we should walk in them—living the good life which He prearranged and made ready for us to live."

"Taking paths prepared" meant that He knew what He was asking me to do and that He knew that I was equipped to do it. I found a promise contained in this verse that meant that He wouldn't put anything greater on me than He put in me. I was catching glimpses of "living the good life which He prearranged." I liked what I saw. "Show me the paths you have for me, Father," I prayed.

I began to see needs. I began to hear about areas of responsibility that were wanting in my church. Yet, I learned to pray that the Lord would raise up the right person to fill each need, all the while remaining open within myself to possibly being that person.

One need that was becoming quite evident was for a program director for the Christmas program. It seemed that everyone who was in leadership who would have naturally picked up that job was planning to be out of town for Christmas since the holiday fell on a Monday. The tradition of the church was that the Christmas program was to be on the Sunday just preceding Christmas. That meant the program was to be on Christmas Eve. I was going to be at home, I had the time, I felt I had the physical strength and God could use whatever talents I had when they were added and blended with the talents of others. With His leading and infusing strength, I knew I could do it. I prayed about the project, discussed it with Lee and then with our pastor. With the enthusiastic support of the pastor and the quiet support of my husband, I officially volunteered to direct the church Christmas program that year.

There had been no supersonic boom from heaven directing me specifically; I was learning that God speaks to us deeply, quietly, within. God doesn't yell and scream to be heard above the noise of our lives, but speaks quietly and gently, beneath it. We don't need to struggle to strain to hear Him, but to rest and quietly listen. He will speak, and we will know it's His voice we are hearing.

I began to have severe attacks of pain and gas in my upper stomach. I did not conduct one practice or workers' meeting without being in intense pain. God really proved that He is strong in our weaknesses. The program was a success. It was a program truly blessed of God and anointed with His Spirit.

It had been determined through tests earlier in the month of December that I had gall-bladder problems and I would need surgery. Soon after the diagnosis, I attended a healing service.

At one point in the service the speaker looked my way, pointed directly at me, and said, "There is a stomach healing taking place right now."

I knew that I was the one referred to, and I went forward to receive it. The speaker started toward me with her arms outstretched as if to hug me. We never actually touched each other, for it was like the opposite ends of a magnet coming toward each other and I ended up on the floor. I felt as if I had somehow been plopped right in the lap of Jesus. I don't know how long I lay there on the floor, but the time I spent there was in perfect praise and adoration for my Lord who, I was sure, had healed my gall bladder.

Then the attacks began to be more intense and the pain became almost violent within my body, and I thought I had misread God. Defeated, I again headed for surgery.

But it was different this time for me. I did not have the same dread, fears, and anxieties. I felt that something good was to happen to me in this time of surgery. I went to sleep peacefully, wondering if it was a rerun of my bypass surgery.

Dr. John was doing the surgery and I had the same anesthetist, I was in the same hospital, under the care of the same nurses. There was the same cart ride to the operating room, and the same recovery room.

RECOVERY ROOM! You mean it's over already?

I had no sensation of choking.

I had no pain except when I laughed. (Really!)

I knew that I would recover quickly.

I did not have, or do not recall having, any hypos after that surgery. I felt very alert. As soon as I was fully awake, that same day I was even concerned about my appearance, and put on a little make-up before my husband came back to see me.

The next day when Dr. John came in, he told me something I had been waiting to hear and didn't even know it. He commented on how well the surgery had gone, and how peacefully I had gone to sleep. Then he said, "By the way, I checked over the surgery we did last year, and your intestines look as if you were born with them that way, and your liver is as clear as a baby's."

"Well, I've got the best surgeon in town, you know," I teased.

"I'm only responsible for the cutting. Someone else is in charge of the healing, and He did a superb job on you," he said.

I was elated. Not only had God forgiven me for having the bypass in the first place, He had used empirical evidence to prove it. My doctor had said it: I was whole and healthy inside. Others had had severe liver problems due to fat, but mine was as clear as a baby's. Others had had problems with scar tissue in the intestinal tract, but not me—I looked like I had been born that way! Praise God! He doeth all things well! I have not had any condemnation about my surgery since that time, and have had much freedom to talk about it. I have met several others since then whom I have been able to share this experience with; they also had the bypass and suffered from condemnation. At last I was sure of God's forgiveness.

God had begun to get the message through to me that I was an okay person and He loved me enough to prove it.

I still lived with disappointment. I did not lose weight at the rapid rate that I had hoped. After a year I had lost only 30 pounds! And after three years, only 60. And, in fact, I was at that time beginning to gain again. When the scale reached 188, I returned to the doctor for help.

"Why haven't I lost more weight?" I asked him. "And why am I gaining?"

"You will have to cut your calorie intake, Neva," he advised.

"But if I could have done that, I wouldn't have had to have the surgery," I moaned. He shrugged his shoulders; and thus I was back on the old road of condemnation again. Why couldn't I cut down on my food intake like other people? Why could everyone else but me diet successfully? I asked myself many more foolish questions that had no answers. Not everyone was dieting successfully. Not everyone was cutting down on food intake.

I decided that I was a hopeless case. But then the Lord finally got through to me. I had found Him so adequate in so many other areas, why not try Him in this area as well?

"Can you help me, God?" was my prayer. "I only fail and enter into condemnation and self-destructive, negative feelings when I try it by myself."

I looked around for a couple of people who might try God's way with me. I was sure I needed the support. I talked to two other people who were having battles with weight following pregnancies, and we began. We dug deep into God's Word and started counting calories. God worked miracles. He taught me that I had eaten for reward, for revenge, for comfort, and a variety of other reasons. So much inner hurt and confusion and rebellion surfaced that I was amazed. I let God deal with problems as they came up and found that I needed less and less to eat. Counting calories brought into my life self-control and discipline which started to benefit other areas of my life as well. Other people began asking how I was losing weight, and I shared on a larger scale than that first small group. Others were losing weight and asked for more Bible studies, and I began writing Bible studies for overweight Christians who wanted to be free of their awful fat life.

What an exciting concept. And Overeaters Victorious

was born! A ministry in addition to the new thinner me! How beautifully God does things when we let Him. Surrender and conquer—give up and win! Strange, yet true.

Being thin is wonderful:

I can reach into the bottom cupboards in the kitchen without getting down on my hands and knees.

I can sit *in* a church pew instead of *on* one.

I can sit beside someone the same height as I without being six inches taller.

I step on an elevator with perfect confidence that it will not shake and scare everyone aboard.

I can get into the back seat of a compact car.

I can buy clothes right off the rack that are made for someone my age.

Would I have the surgery again? Surgery is not the answer. Jesus is the answer.

God has revealed to me that my eating habits were carnal, or fleshly, and the source of many of my spiritual battles. However, I also learned that in Him there is victory! Previously I had made Jesus Lord in every area except my mouth.

I still have struggles, but not without hope, for Jesus is Lord. I can do all things through Him who gives me strength; not will power—strength.

I believe that I was healed at that healing service, but in a very unique way, for God always does things uniquely. I believe that God removed the scars in my intestines and cleared my liver that night on the floor of the meeting room. I believe that during the beautiful experience there, He performed supernatural surgery to prove, without a doubt, His forgiveness for the bypass. And not only did He perform that surgery on my body, He did a radical on my self-image and healed many of the injuries I had sustained in that area. I have not been the same since—in my attitude toward God, myself, or in my response toward others. It truly was a turning point in my life.

Chapter eleven

I had a very low self-image and my weight problem was only one way in which it showed up.

There was a day when a dear friend dropped in on me without calling first and I apologized for the mess. I began picking up newspapers that ten minutes before had not even bothered me.

I flitted,
 I fluttered,
  I fussed, and
   I fumed.

Her response to this sudden busyness was: "What is the matter, Neva? Don't you accept yourself as you are? I do, and I love you."

I have always had some trouble with organizing my house, and I have sometimes let housework challenge me instead of my challenging it. For years I dreaded the thought that someone might drop in on me and find me in a mess. I am an arts-and-crafts person. Most of my projects are made on the dining room table. Since my dining room and living room are adjacent, with no wall in between, I might as well have a workshop in my living room.

At the same time, I wanted everyone who knew me to think I was a perfect housekeeper. In order to keep up that image, I wouldn't get too close to people; I didn't care to have friends who were on "dropping-in terms." This did two things to me. First, it denied me the right to be myself. Second, it denied me close friends.

When I did entertain, even simply, I worked entirely too

hard just cleaning my house. It was not really worth the effort. Gradually I came to a day when I said, "Enough of this. I am who I am, and if no one else ever loved me, so what? God does, and His love is proving to be sufficient."

I began to do things out of love, not obligation, and I found that living became much easier for me. My attitude about the house has changed, and things are getting better.

You see, there was change, but it came through accepting myself as I was.

In Sunday school class discussions, one often hears remarks like: "Well, the way it looks to me . . ." or "I think that . . ." or "In my opinion . . ." but those kinds of prefaces were always made by other people. I usually began my remarks with "Don't you think that . . .?" or "Wouldn't you say that . . .?" or "Is it possible that . . .?" I did not think enough of my own opinion to take credit or blame for it. I looked for someone else with whom to share the responsibilty.

This characteristic was very revealing to some other Christians who brought it to my attention: I came to realize that I was entitled to my opinion, my own thoughts, and my own perspective. I had to learn that I was a person of
opinions,
likes and dislikes,
and also biases;
but everyone is,
and this beautiful variety fits into
God's plan.

Through daily study of God's Word and prayer, I have come to see many other things about myself. God wanted me to look at who I was and what I was, not what I *thought* I was or who I thought I was. Many of our old hymns have verses in them that say such things as "such a worm as I," and I had heard many preachers remind us that "we're just sinners, saved by grace." I believe they should tell us that we *were* sinners but now we're children of the King! When I saw in God's Word that we are "the righteousness of God in Christ," "His workmanship," a gift of God to Christ, I began to see myself from God's perspective.

I think a better analogy than "worm" is caterpillar. I had woven a cocoon tightly around me by my carnal practices and deceit. But now it was a new season—a season for release. I wasn't very much a caterpillar anymore; I was becoming a butterfly. Instead of being stuck to some tree branch being tossed about in the wind, I was now seeing life from a new perspective. I was learning to rise above situations and circumstances to soar to my full potential. Life was so beautiful. I was not the "somebody" I had been before. Now I was becoming the real me, the somebody God intended.

I found the courage in Christ to look at who I wanted to be and what I wanted to be and not get hung up on the fact that I had not arrived there as yet. I came to the realization that though I had not yet become all that God wanted me to be, that together we were working on it. I will become all that He can enable me to be, according to how much freedom I give Him to do so.

I have a little button that says "PBPGINFWMY." It means: "Please Be Patient, God Is Not Finished With Me Yet." "Praise God!" Ephesians 2:10 says the same thing, "We *are* His workmanship. . ." (present tense, referring to an ongoing and lifelong process).

I once saw a little plaque which read: "God made me, and He don't make no junk!"

I can straighten my spine and stand tall. I will hold my head high. I'm no junk. I'm a daughter of the King.

In accepting myself just as I am, I have found that people are more comfortable with me, and I am more comfortable with me, and I am more comfortable with people. When I don't put on a front, they let down their walls, too.

This is honesty, and it is contagious. It is so much easier for me to be me, and you to be you.

It's so simple:
"You be honest with me,
   and I'll be honest with you!"
This has its risks, I know. You may not like me as much if you thought I was perfect—but then, you'll never worship me either, or put me on a pedestal. But then again, I'll not be able to question your motives if you take me for what I am either.

Someone told me that I would have to face the fact that not everyone would like me; but if I liked myself more, it would not matter as much.

In order to like myself more, I had to learn where I was biased, where I was strong, and where I was weak.

I have to ask myself over and over if those weaknesses and biases affect my point of view, shape my opinion, and color my decisions.

I could look at the world and all those in it realistically once I was aware of my own biases. Many of my biases have not changed, and probably will not change, but I can use them to bring about reality in my outlook instead of hiding from reality behind them. Nor can I let my biases allow me to be unkind or unloving.

When I am speaking and teaching, it is really important that I have an accurate self-image. When God uses me and I am aware of my own strengths and weaknesses, God's power moving through me is much more clearly evident, and it prevents me from taking to myself the glory that rightfully belongs to Him. When I am speaking or teaching a Bible study, for instance, I am aware that someone with my limited ability and experience has absolutely nothing to say, apart from God, to those listening, expecting, and waiting to learn.

Whatever they hear has to be from God, and I put myself in neutral so God in me can be put in gear. Then He
   blesses me,
      teaches me,
         and uses me—for others.

Chapter twelve

What a joy it is to have the responsibility of praying daily for another person. God chose this method to demonstrate to me how He sometimes expresses His love for His children. Let me explain.

A few years ago our church announced the need for volunteer prayer partners to back up our youth choir with prayer support. I was assigned the name of a young medical student. I came to love him very much and to watch him grow in the Lord, marry and move away. I have never had to remind myself to pray for him and his lovely young wife. God brings them to mind, I pray, and soon I hear from them. It seems that the times I have been most burdened for them are the times they have been facing decisions of one kind or another. They have borne so much in moving out-of-state and into the hectic routine of a surgical resident's schedule. God used this experience to show me how much He loves His children. "Hey, I'm one of them, too." The realization almost surprised me.

If I am faithful to pray when He lays someone on my heart, could it be that He has others praying in the same way for me? I dared to believe it to be true.

And then people began to say to me: "I have had you on my mind; are you feeling all right?" "I prayed for you this week. How's it going?" "I love you."

All that blew my mind.

I loved it,
    and them,
        and God.

Two of man's greatest needs are to love and to be loved.

I've always known that, but I thought I had to *feel* love. I discovered, though, that love isn't something you feel; it's something you do. A friend told me, "If you want to love someone, do loving things for them—then the feeling comes." I had thought the reverse to be true.

I looked back over the past few years and realized that is what I had done during the crisis time before our son's birth. I had been so afraid my husband was going to leave me that I began to do loving things. I began to listen to his opinion, to let him voice his opinion in a group without my doing it for him.

I was in for a shock when I began to really listen to him; I found that I liked what I heard. I gave more effort to our relationship and, as a result, I fell in love with my own husband. It was different than what I had experienced in our relationship before.

I found that I was able to express love to my husband without any strings attached to it. This kind of love did not demand that he love me back in the same way that I loved him. But it left him free to discover and express his love for me also in new and exciting ways.

I loved my children more. I became more patient with them. I enjoyed them more. I think they enjoyed me more, too. Playing with them, training and teaching them jobs around the house were no longer a chore. I loved to sew for them and sing to them and all the other things that I thought only mothers in Sunday school papers did.

I found that this new kind of love, which had been beyond my own capabilities, flowed freely through Jesus Christ living in me and through me; the kind of life He desired of me and for me was becoming a reality.

I saw a further parallel to my marital relationship and my relationship with Christ. Both marriage and the born-again experience found in Christ are institutions of God. I saw that with both comes a committal to one special way of life, which means turning from any other. Turning from all others and committal to one person is a deliberate choice made by myself upon the invitation of another.

God places a lot of value upon my relationship both with Christ and with my husband, and through them He makes provision for all my needs.

In Christ I have:
    salvation,
        the filling with the Holy Spirit,
            power to live His way,
                power to witness,
                    and eternal life.

In my husband I have found, through God's principles applied in my life:
    completion,
        protection,
            provision,
                and a loving atmosphere which cushions me
                    from the pressures of the world.

In both relationships I find
    a place to grow,
        a place to rest,
            a place to love,
                a place to give,
                    a place of complete fulfillment.

In Ephesians 5:2 are found these words, "Walk in love—esteeming and delighting in one another. . . ."

What does that mean, Lord?

What are you saying?

It sounds like a purposeful, deliberate kind of life, where life doesn't just happen as each day comes; rather, it is anticipated, and the new day comes full of promise and potential instead of dread and fear. It sounded very much like a section of scripture in Proverbs 4:25-27 which had encouraged me to begin to set goals in my life.

I asked God to reveal to me the kind of love He wanted me to have in my marriage, and I can't tell you even half of

His revelation. It really is above all that I could ask or even think!

At first, planning the walk of love seemed to be a lot of work. "How can I do this by myself?" I pray. "You can't," God answers. "But I can, in you and through you." Why, it's a brand-new life!

It didn't take me long to learn that my efforts at walking in love toward my husband demanded a love that I was not capable of giving on my own. Many times I did not have the kind of love that was required. My love tended to be
conditional,
    self-centered,
        and shabby,
compared to the kind I wanted in the love relationship for my marriage. Now what was I to do? God was requiring of me a love that I couldn't possibly give without Him constantly supplying His love to me. A love that was
free of jealousy,
    pure and gentle,
        full of mutual understanding,
            patient,
                and boundless.

"You're going to have to take over some of these attitudes, Lord. Show me how you want your love expressed to Lee today, Father, through me."

The first area He started on was a very strange one, but I learned the lesson because God came quickly to the point.

I had, in my early days of marriage, thought that if I treated Lee the way I wanted to be treated, he would get the message and return the favor. So, on special occasions, I bought him romantic and "mushy" cards. He bought the contemporary type for me.

I felt very insulted with funny cards, because I felt he should spend hours poring over the card racks searching for just the one that would express his passionate love for me. And he merely put the card exclaiming my undying love and devotion in his dresser drawer.

I felt crushed.

"What's wrong, God?" I asked one day. And He showed me. I was treating him according to my need, not his own.

The Bible says, "Do unto others as you would have them do unto you," and I thought that meant since I like mushy cards I should buy one for him. But it doesn't.

It means to treat him according to *his* needs and desires, and he will respond to your needs and desires. He likes funny cards; so now I buy him funny cards. Now he buys me mushy cards. I love mushy cards.

It works better this way, and the message gets across— we love each other. And we don't just depend on the verse of the card to tell each other so, either!

I learned to admire him. It wasn't easy, for I felt very uncomfortable with this at first. First of all, I hadn't looked closely enough at him to find things to admire. I thought love was enough, and I could express that easily in words. Now I have a clearer understanding of how hard it was for him, at first, to express his love for me in words, just like it was hard for me to express my admiration. But I needed his love expressed, and he needed my admiration. Now we are doing pretty well, for I am doing unto him as I would have him do unto me.

"Please, God," I had prayed, "you teach me about love." He did. He gives me love, and then I give it to my husband and to my children.

I give it to my neighbors. I even have some left over, so I give it back to Him. Then He gives me more love, and the whole process starts over and over and over again. I always have a fresh supply now, and it does not depend on how my husband loves me, or my children talk to me, or my neighbors treat me. It all depends on God as long as I depend on Him. I found that He is dependable.

It's no longer a chore to be a Christian. It is an adventure!

Chapter thirteen

One of the surest ways I know of staying strong and keeping my faith in God up-to-date and vitally relevant to my life is to reproduce Christ's character in others. It should be as natural as any reproduction cycle in any other part of life. When I first had the deep desire to lead someone else to Jesus, I wanted this one to be someone who could see results and changes as I had seen in my life. Also, I wanted to be used in the whole process—

planting the seed,
tending the field,
and reaping the harvest.

But it scared me to death. I had often quieted this desire in me and tried to be content with just praying with people when they came to the altar at our church. However, there were so many outside our church who never would kneel at an altar in church, and so I realized that I was going to have to reach out.

I stood at that same window in the living room again and this time looked across the bay to the houses lined up on the opposite shore. I began to pray for this one and that. I watched their lights go on in the mornings of winter; and I imagined people being saved and lighting up little lights in heaven.

"O God," I would pray, "make me effective for you. Reach out through me and touch the lives of my neighbors."

I bought a good book one day when I was shopping in a Christian bookstore. I was delighted with the purchase because I had responded to a nudge from God, and I knew He was going to use it somehow. I put it on the dashboard of the car and waited for Him to give the next step.

I went over to a neighbor's to pick up my daughter who had been there playing, and as I started to get out of the car I felt it.

"This is it," God said. "Give this book to the young mother here."

"But, God!" I objected. "This is not one of the neighbors I have been praying for. I don't even know Joy too well. We just met and, God, do you want her to think I'm a religious fanatic just when we are first getting acquainted?"

I heard no reply, but I felt God's finger right in the middle of my back pushing me toward the front door of my new friend's house. Clutched in my hand was the book.

"Hi," she said. "The kids have been having a great time. I hope they can get together again soon."

Not when you see what I'm going to give you, I thought. I shoved the book into my coat pocket, helped put the coats on the girls, and headed them toward the door.

"It's now or never," God said.

I turned quickly, startling my friend and pushed the book at her. "Here's a book you might like," I said. I got out of there as fast as possible. I was afraid that she would either throw me and the book out together or call me a fanatic to my face. I began to pray for her with much fervency.

Finally God told me that I would have to face her—the "tending-the-field" stage. One day the phone rang.

"Hello," I said into the receiver.

"Hi, Neva?"

"Yes."

"Could I come over?" she asked. "I want to have you pray for my church."

"Your church?" I said. I silently prayed, "I don't want to pray for her church, God; I want to pray for her."

"Well, we've been having a few problems there, and you're the first person I thought of when I thought of having someone pray for it with me."

"Well, okay," I said. I felt the finger of God in my back again.

"I'll be right over," she said and hung up.

I hurried about the house picking up a few things here and there (more habit than anything else by now). I located my Bible and sat down a minute to be quiet before she came. I asked God what was going on. I had asked Him to bring my neighbors to Him through me; but their churches? Before God could answer, the doorbell rang.

"Come on in, Joy," I said, answering the door. "Let's go into the dining room. The sun is shining in the window and it's wonderful sitting in the warmth."

We went into the dining room and sat at the table. She began to share a few problems she was experiencing at her church, while all the time I wondered, "What are you telling me this for?"

After a while she stopped and took a deep breath. "I guess I'm not really here to have you pray for my church, after all; I think I'm the one who needs prayer. Will you pray for me?"

"*You?*" I asked innocently, while saying to God under my breath, "Now I see what you are doing."

"What do you want me to pray for, Joy?"

"I think I want the baptism with the Holy Spirit," she said.

"What? Are you sure?" I asked. "O Lord, help us all," I whispered to God.

Now, I had experienced this for myself, but I wasn't sure I was supposed to pass it around. I wasn't really selfish, but I wasn't sure, either. I didn't know if she had ever accepted Jesus as her Savior as yet, and it bothered me to think that the first person I ever really brought to Jesus, face to face, might be getting the cart before the horse. "Now what?" I prayed silently, in panic. "God, I don't even know if she is born again. Do something!"

There I sat, with my new friend and neighbor, holding her hand, enduring the longest silence I had ever endured. I couldn't think of anything to pray. She started praying for herself.

"Lord," she said, "I don't know if you are in my heart or not, and I'm not sure how to get you there." I knew it was my turn to do something evangelical and clever so she would be won. Right? Wrong! I couldn't think of anything to say or pray. So she went on at last.

"I don't know how to ask you there, but I do know how to sing you there." And with that statement, and me in shock, she began, with tears streaming down her cheeks, a song I had learned in Sunday school, just like she had:

"Into my heart, into my heart,
Come into my heart, Lord Jesus.
Come in today.
Come in to stay.
Come into my heart, Lord Jesus."

Then, as if that wasn't enough for one day, she continued: "Now, Lord, I want to receive the Holy Spirit." And nothing happened.

I was in agony. I knew I had blown it. My first convert, and I had blown it! "Receive it by faith," I told her, and quickly related how I had received a prayer language when I was alone the next day. That satisfied her, and she left thanking me, laughing, praising God—and I felt I had blown it.

She called me sometime later and confirmed that she had received her praise and prayer language. She was ecstatic, but I still felt that I had blown it.

I asked God about it, and the answer was simple:

I hadn't done it at all. He had done it. We never win anyone. God does it. We are only used. He is the one who does it all. "Thank you, Jesus!" I prayed. "I blew it, and you knew it. But you did it anyway, and let me watch. You are so great!"

The next day the same neighbor called and asked me if I could pray with another neighbor, and I thought, "Here we go again." I said okay to them, but to God I said, "Since you are going to do it your own way, why don't you just take over from the beginning? And He did.

He taught me in just two short days how to lead someone to Him: Just let Him do it. Through me, yes, but He does it.

The second neighbor has also received Christ, and the changes in these two neighbors' lives have been just beautiful to watch. They have become two of my closest friends, and we can

pray together,
    study together,
        share together.
            And a time or two, we have suffered together.
There is a little poem which says:

"God is great.
 God is Good.
 God lives in our neighborhood."

And I know what that means to me.

There was another young nurse who lived with us for a while after she completed her training. Due to struggles and problems in my life as well as hers, we had drifted apart after her marriage. She attended our former church.

While I was in the hospital for my gall-bladder surgery, she came up to see me, for she was working in the same hospital.

"Well, Linda," I said as I recognized the familiar face peeking from behind the curtain stretched around my bed.

"Hi," she said. "You up to having company?"

"Sure." I was getting excited about seeing her again after two years.

"I heard you were here when I came on duty,"

"Duty? Are you working on this floor?"

"No, I'm on Four tonight, but you know you're well known here," she teased. "The word gets around fast when our favorite patients return."

"This is the last time I'll be here," I said. "This is the last thing that could possibly go wrong."

"Well, I don't know about that, but I didn't come to talk about your physical condition. I'll let the nurses on your case worry about that."

"Good," I said. "Let's just visit and catch up on things. How are the kids? and your husband?"

"They're just fine."

"How's everything at church?" I asked cautiously.

"Just the same." She lowered her gaze to her lap and continued, "You are happy, aren't you?"

"Yes," I said.

"I thought so. I can tell by just talking to you that things are going well. You seem so happy and content, even with all this taking place."

"Linda, Jesus is real to me. At last I've come to know Him in a real and positive way."

"That's good to hear, Neva," she smiled at me. "My break time is over, but can I come back and talk some more later?"

"Sure you can. I'll count on it."

It was in those brief visits in the hospital that we found the paths of our lives coming together again.

I carefully shared the new joy I had found in my walk with Jesus, and the power I had longed for for so long. She was thoughtful, and after my release she began to call me. We talked about the doctrine we both had been raised with, carefully examined it, and encouraged each other with all the good things about the church in which we had been brought up. Though I was no longer a member of that church, I will always feel a part of it, since that is where I accepted Jesus as my Savior.

"Lord," I prayed, "please work through me to reach Linda and reinforce your love for her. Thank you for the love I feel for her and her family. If you want her to learn the things I have learned, please let me keep my personality out of the way so that your personality shines through. I can't do anything without you. I've found that out the hard way. I take my hands off and submit to the Holy Spirit. You give me the words to speak. I trust you. Thank you."

We shared many times together after that and God did not let me down. We asked each other questions in our search of the Scriptures, and God would seem to direct our attention to just the right passages for answers. I did not have to come up with even one answer on my own. He was right there all the time. He brought scriptures to memory. He used my own experiences and Linda's desire to know Him in His fullness. It wasn't long before Linda was experiencing the new walk in the Spirit for herself, the same that I had entered a year earlier. She came with a spring in her step and a twinkle in her eyes; and she was so in love with Jesus, her husband, her children and her life—and me, her friend—that she has not been the same since.

God had answered my prayer.

There is something about the Spirit-filled life that acts like a magnet to those around us; and Linda's friends became drawn to Jesus through her in much the same way as mine had through me. Jesus was making an appearance on the scene in a magnificent way.

She has since moved away, and I miss her very much. I know that Jesus always brings someone else to take the place of those He moves away, and He will certainly have to go some to top this very special friend in my life.

There have been other instances where God has chosen to work through me to reach others. Not that I am special, because I'm not any different from any other person; but I've chosen to be available. I have elected to let Him do it. I have learned to use my talents but not to rely on them.

I've seen God reach out to others in special places—in an airplane, in my home town, in the hospital, in the grocery store, in a Bible study, and in many other unusual places as well. I had a sneaking suspicion that God worked in many other places besides church, and I was right. He does. He'll work wherever people simply cry out to Him.

Chapter fourteen

I have learned that God speaks to me through His Word. If I read it daily, not legalistically but faithfully, I can have a running commentary with Him and He teaches me many things. I receive answers to the problems at hand and God uses this time with Him to show me areas in which He desires to deal with me or to free me.

To illustrate, I was reading in 2 Corinthians one day and not really absorbing what I had read. I have days when I have to rely on Him by faith to teach me something, because the words I read seem to "go in one ear and out the other." It was a day like that. All of a sudden one verse seemed to reach out of the page and grab my attention. I reread it: "Casting down imaginations, and every high thing that exalteth itself against the knowledge of God, and bringing into captivity every thought to the obedience of Christ" (2 Cor. 10:5, KJV).

"Hold it, God," I said, "I haven't the slightest idea what you are talking about here."

I started to meditate on that first phrase, "casting down imaginations." My mother has often told me that I have a fine mind and a wild imagination. I always had imaginary friends when I didn't have anyone to play with, and I could fantasize by the hour in my adolescent years. I am interested in all sorts of creative activities, including painting, music, writing, drama, and all the rest. I thought that imaginations were creative in origin and that they were not things to be "cast down."

"Am I getting warm?" I asked God.

"Keep going," God seemed to say.

"Let's see, now. What do I imagine now?"

"What about imaginary fears?" God said.

"I don't have any imaginary fears, God. They are all real."

"Are they?" He continued. "What about when I said, 'There is no fear in love; but perfect love casteth out fear: because fear hath torment. He that feareth is not made perfect in love'?" (1 John 4:18).

"Well, I know that sometimes I get carried away and think that things are going to happen."

"What do you experience then?"

"Fear, Lord," I confessed.

I began to see the point of this conversation with God. Could it be that I could live without this fear? I could see that it was possible if I were willing to open my thought life to God. I needed to confess as sin my habit of dwelling on thoughts and imaginations that led me into a state of fear. I reflected on the times when I thought that my husband would be killed in a car accident on the way to or from work. I have many times waited in agony for him to come home, even if he were only fifteen minutes later than usual. I could truly see that the phrase in the 18th verse of 1 John 4, "fear hath torment," was really true. I came to see that I could live without this fear.

One day about that time I had to leave the house just a few minutes before my daughters' school bus arrived to take them off to school for the day. As I drove around the shoreline road to take my son to nursery school, the fear thoughts began their invasion. "Someone will kidnap your girls. That's what you get for leaving them alone out on the edge of the road. Not only will someone steal them, but they will be brutally molested as well." I was almost paralyzed with fear. I grew cold, and perspiration collected on my face and in my palms. "How could you leave them home alone for such terrible things to happen to them? You will never be able to forgive yourself, and your husband will never forgive you either. . . . You call yourself a Christian mother, and yet you can so easily shove your responsibilities aside. Boy, you'd better take another look at yourself."

I dropped off my son at the nursery school and quickly drove back home. By the time I got home I was almost sick. The bus stop was empty—they were nowhere in sight. Should I call the school? Would they think I was nuts? What should I do?

"Sandra's glasses!" They were in plain sight on the kitchen table. "I have to take them to school. She can't get along without them for the day!" I said aloud in the empty house. I hurried to school and to my daughter's classroom.

"Hi, Mom," she greeted me in a cheery voice. "I would have called you, but you told us that our responsibility is to remember our belongings and to take them to school or suffer the consequences of forgetting!" I could hear my own words coming out of the mouth of my eight-year-old.

"I know, sweetie, but I was worried." I felt weak.

I quickly kissed her and walked away.

I could see what had happened to me as I left the school and drove home. Not only had I been paralyzed by fear, but I had let the whole situation rule me so that I had gone back on one of the rules I had set up to teach my children a sense of responsibility. (They have had to wear snow boots all day a few times because of forgetting their tennis shoes. They have had to borrow lunch tickets because they have forgotten to take the lunch money set out for them. But even though they felt they were suffering great injustice at the time, they are learning responsibility; and I haven't been put in the trap of running to school with forgotten library books and the rest of the things children use to get mothers running to school.)

"What is this all about, God?" I begged through tears after returning home. "What happened to me?"

"You didn't cast down the imagination when it first started."

"Imagination!" I was disgusted. I sat at the table, put

my head down on my arms and prayed. "God, I tried to deal with this imagination in my own way. I can see now that your ways and my ways, while coming together, are still very far apart. Teach me, Father."

"The weapons of your warfare are not carnal, but mighty through God to the pulling down of strongholds, Neva. I want you to begin to learn how to use spiritual weapons."

"You mean like the sword of the Spirit?"

"Yes, Neva. My Word."

I read again the section (2 Cor. 10:3-5, KJV).

"For though we walk in the flesh, we do not war after the flesh: (for the weapons of our warfare are not carnal, but mighty through God to the pulling down of strong holds;) casting down imaginations, and every high thing that exalteth itself against the knowledge of God, and bringing into captivity every thought to the obedience of Christ."

And 1 John 4:18: "There is no fear in love; but perfect love casteth out fear; because fear hath torment. He that feareth is not made perfect in love."

Since that day I remember that verse when those times of attack come. God's love is perfect, and in His love there is no fear.

I have learned to handle unclean thoughts in this same way, too. Unclean thoughts are included in that which "exalteth itself against the knowledge of God."

I have learned to pray a simple little prayer now. And it helps: "Father, I have this unclean thought (or imagination). This is not my thought, for I stand before you in the name of Jesus and disown it. I am your child, God, and I trust you to deal with it and to take it away. I rest in Jesus."

For a while the thoughts persisted and the imaginations continued. They started coming in the forms of nightmares and bad dreams. I prayed the prayer again. The thoughts went away. Then they came again. I prayed again—the same prayer over and over again. Finally they came with less and less frequency. I pray that little prayer every time I experience this type of satanic attack. God is faithful. As I use scripture and let God work in my life through a knowledge of His Word, I find that I am able to use those weapons, which are not carnal, with efficiency and effect.

"Help me, God, in my thought life, too. I tried to clean up my mind, and I just became confused. Help me, Father. I can't do it by myself."

He does it every time.

I pray this little prayer at other times, too.

When I think I'm misunderstood;
  When I think I'm too fat for anyone to like;
    (My body is thinner, but some of my thoughts are still fat.)
      When I think someone is talking
        about me;
        When I think nobody loves me.

God hears it. He honors it, and I am free from the thoughts that would
  scare me,
    depress me,
      distress me,
        and otherwise drive a wedge between
          God and me.
  "Help me, God.
    "I'm yours.
      "I surrender to you."
        That's all it takes.

Chapter fifteen

I do not mean to imply that I have been the only one to
    change,
        grow,
            and mature.
My husband has, too. He has really become
    a beautiful person,
        growing in the Lord,
            learning His ways,
                assuming his position as
                    head of the home.
Our love is
    deeper,
        newer,
            brighter,
                freer,
                    and rooted in Jesus.
Lee received the baptism with the Holy Spirit very soon
after I did, and the difference in him is
    beautiful
        welcome,
            and just what I needed.
Every morning he puts his arms around me and prays
for me,
    for my day,
        for my Bible study, if I am to teach,
            and he tells God that
                he appreciates me and loves me,
                    and praises God for giving me to him.

Then he kisses me and tells me he loves me—and I start every day on Cloud Nine.

My relationship with our children is much different, too. They have become little people to me instead of possessions. They need training in the ways of God, and as He trains me, I pass it on. I make them obey, because God requires obedience, instead of my being threatened if they don't; and it alters my method.

Instead of spanking and yelling, it is spanking and hugging, repentance and forgiveness. Instead of handing out punishment, we administer correction—which all adds up to freedom from tension

in them,

in Lee,

and in me.

Being a mother is much more fun than it used to be since I prayed, and surrendered it all to Him: "Help me, God. I tried it alone, without you, and I messed the whole thing up. If you don't help me, it won't get done. I can't do it without you."

I have told my story for several reasons. One is to remind me of how good God is to me and how He has worked in my life. Another is to tell you how good God wants to be to you, too.

I took a long, round-about journey beginning with accepting Jesus as Savior and declaring Him as Lord. And it cost me a lot. It need not cost you the time, sickness, and insecurity it cost me.

God did not intend to have me go this route into His perfect will for my life. I determined that myself. My church did not get me off the track. I did it myself. My growth is my responsibility. I was

stubborn,

willful,

extravagant,

distrustful,

and miserable.

But, as the songwriter puts it,

"Something beautiful, something good.
All my confusion, He understood.
All I had to offer Him
Was brokenness and strife.
But He made something beautiful
Out of my life."*

Your life can be beautiful, too.
God did it for me, and
He'll do it for you.
Just ask Him.

You, too, can be free of your cocoon. God desires that all of us rise to our full potential, giving us wings like the butterfly. I am free because I chose to leave the cocoon. I'm living free.

---

*From the song, "Something Beautiful" by Bill Gaither. Used with permission.

Books by Neva Coyle:

Free To Be Thin, w/Marie Chapian, a successful weight-loss plan which links learning how to eat with how to live

There's More To Being Thin Than Being Thin, w/Marie Chapian, focusing on the valuable lessons learned on the *journey* to being thin

Slimming Down and Growing Up, w/Marie Chapian, applying the "Free To Be Thin" principles to kids

Living Free, her personal testimony

Daily Thoughts on Living Free, a devotional

Scriptures for Living Free, a counter-top display book of Scriptures to accompany the devotional

Free To Be Thin Cookbook, a collection of tasty, nutritious recipes complete with the calorie content of each

Free To Be Thin Leader's Kit, a step-by-step guide for organizing and leading an Overeaters Victorious group, including five cassette tapes of instruction

Free To Be Thin Daily Planner, a three-month planner for recording daily thoughts, activities and calorie intake

Tape Albums and Study Guides by Neva Coyle:

(The study guides come with the tape albums but may also be ordered separately.)

A Seminar on Living Free (four cassettes) A recording of her seminar in which she shares the principles that have helped her break free from a life of misery and self-satisfaction
Living Free Study Guide, to accompany the tape album

Free To Be Thin (seven cassettes) Victory, Weight-loss, Deliverance
Free To Be Thin Study Guide No. 1, Getting Started, to be used with the book by the same title, and/or the tape album

Discipline (four cassettes) A Program for Spiritual Fitness
Free To Be Thin Study Guide No. 2, Discipline, to be used with the book by the same title, and/or the tape album

Abiding (four cassettes) Honesty in Relationships
Abiding Study Guide

Freedom (four cassettes) Escape from the Ordinary
Freedom Study Guide

Diligence (four cassettes) Overcoming Discouragement
Diligence Study Guide

Obedience (four cassettes) Developing a Listening Heart
Obedience Study Guide

Free To Be Thin Aerobics, available in LP record album with booklet, or cassette tape album with booklet

Restoration (Four cassettes) Helping restore those who may have faltered in their spiritual life or commitment
Restoration Study Guide

For information regarding OVEREATERS VICTORIOUS and for current price lists on other materials, send a business-size, stamped, self-addressed envelope to Overeaters Victorious, Inc., P.O. Box 179, Redlands, CA 92373.

If you would like to receive special mailings concerning Overeaters Victorious seminars in your area, fill out the form below. (*Allow four weeks.*)

Name _____

Address _____

City/State _____ Zip _____